EDWARDIAN
HOUSE STYLE

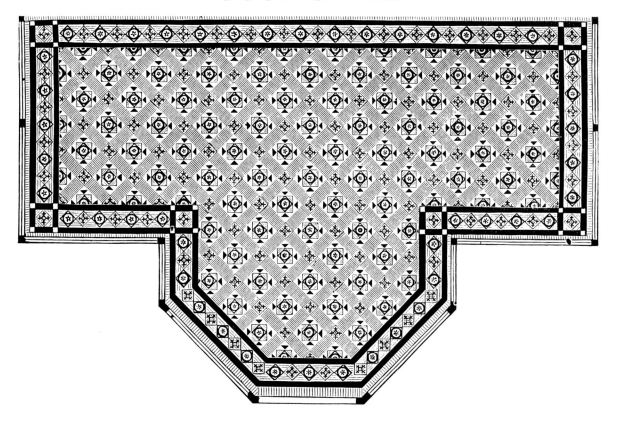

AN ARCHITECTURAL AND INTERIOR DESIGN SOURCE BOOK

EDWARDIAN HOUSE STYLE

AN ARCHITECTURAL AND INTERIOR DESIGN SOURCE BOOK

HILARY MANDLEBERG

David & Charles

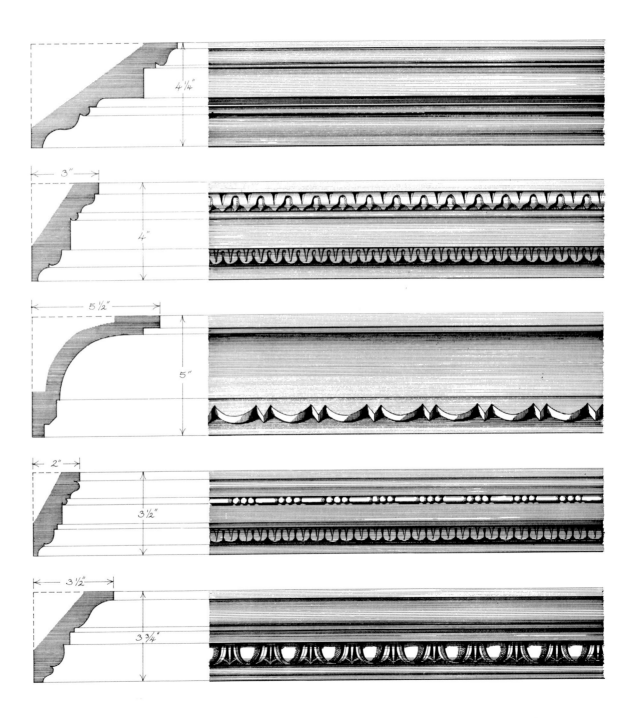

Contents

W.C.M. 88

W.C.M. 89

W.C.M. 90

W.C.M. 91.

W.C.M. 92.

W.C.M 93

Introduction

'...so long as the new style had been a matter which in practice concerned only the wealthier class, England could foot the bill. As soon as the problem began to embrace the people as a whole, other nations took the lead, nations that lived no longer, or had never lived, in the atmosphere of the ancien regime, nations that did not accept or did not know England's educational and social contrasts between the privileged classes and those in the suburbs and slums.'

Nikolaus Pevsner, Pioneers of Modern Design, 1960

OPPOSITE PAGE AND BELOW: *Eager to suggest that they had ancestral roots going back generations, the 'new rich' middle class of the turn of the century sometimes decorated their houses with spurious plasterwork and terracotta heraldic devices. Seeing ornately decorated crests topped with feathers suggestive of the Prince of Wales's device, or quartered coats-of arms, passers-by might be forgiven for thinking they were looking at the ancestral home of a long-established family.*

When Edward VII came to the throne in 1901 England was a deeply class-ridden society and for each class of people there were very different sorts of housing. The upper, landed classes could indulge in the changing fashions for the design and decoration of their homes, fashions which they shared with the rich of Europe and America alike. During the nineteenth century, the wealthy tried out a host of different styles. In 1873, Jacob von Falke, one observer at the International Exhibition in Vienna, commented that 'In so far as style is concerned, the modern Frenchman dwells in the eighteenth century, he sleeps in the century likewise, but he dines in the sixteenth, then on occasion smokes his cigar and enjoys his coffee in the Orient, while he takes his bath in Pompeii, in Ancient Greece.'

However, changes were round the corner which were to permeate the social structure, influence people's expectations and affect the way they designed and decorated their homes. For the upper, landed classes in England came the warning that life as they knew it in their comfortable country houses was on the wane. Such people held the firm belief that money invested in land was safe. Then in the 1880s came an influx of cheap corn from America. The result was a drop in demand for English corn and twenty years' depression in English farming. This spelt catastrophe for upper-class families dependent on land. They were suddenly forced to find other ways of making money, by selling off small parts of their property and investing in shares, by sending their sons to work in the City, by sitting as directors on company boards, or by marrying the daughters of the new rich, the wealthy industrialists and bankers.

At the other end of the social spectrum the very poor were also affected by the depression. Farm labourers had to leave their traditional work and seek new employment in the towns. A life of cramped, one-room squalor without proper sanitation was what country labourers always expected but now, with so many leaving the country for the town in search of work, it was very much the way of life for the poor in the towns too. The population of Greater London grew from 3,900,000 in 1871 to an oppressive 7,300,000 in 1911.

To relieve this situation, the 1890s and 1900s saw the first provision of municipal flats and suburban housing for the poor. However, this apparent improvement resulted in many poor people losing their homes when the slums were cleared to provide the new housing. By 1912, the London County Council had displaced nearly half as many people as it rehoused, while the new homes were unaffordable for many of the poorest.

Yet it was the rise of the middle classes that brought about the greatest change and had the most dramatic effect on housing. From 1881 to 1911 another million people were employed in middle- or lower-middle-class jobs. The population was better educated and with the growth of industry and government activity the work was available. As people rose from the lower class to the middle, so they naturally adopted middle-class aspirations. As J. B. Priestley put it in *The Edwardians*, 'Just as the upper middle class were afraid of dangerous ideas, the lower middle class lived in fear of sliding back into the jungles

and bogs of the workers. It had achieved respectability and was terrified of losing it.' One sign of respectability was a decent home. The 'des. res.' of the Victorian age had become discredited and was now regarded as gloomy and uncomfortable. What the new class of consumers wanted were affordable and manageable-sized homes within commuting distance of their work in the cities and towns.

Flats were one possibility. Unpopular in Victorian times when they were associated with housing for the poor, they gradually became more acceptable. Home-making manuals of 1900 to 1920 carried articles on the advantages and disadvantages of flats and maisonettes, recommended how to furnish them, how to protect them from burglary and how to accommodate one's servants in them.

Yet the majority of middle-class people still preferred a house and for most, renting was the only possibility. Building societies would only advance 75 per cent of the purchase price of a home and for people lacking inherited wealth, the prospects of finding the balance were slim. Then, in 1904, the Secretary of the Halifax Building Society offered mortgages of up to 90 per cent on homes valued at less than £200. The floodgates were opened for the middle classes to join the ranks of the property-owners. At that price, decent semi-detached and terraced houses with a garden and a frontage of 16 to 20 feet could be built.

The paraphernalia of Edwardian interiors covered the range from Art Nouveau-inspired jardinieres and umbrella stands to clocks and barometers with classical details.

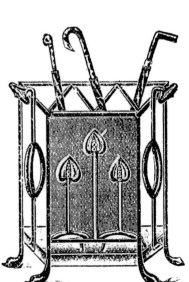

Speculative builders set about meeting the need, building row upon row of terraced and semi-detached houses. As space ran out near town and city centres, people moved to the suburbs, and these quickly became synonymous with the English middle class.

It was precisely the homes of this English middle class that the German Hermann Muthesius came to study in the last years of the nineteenth century. Sent to England as cultural attaché to the German Embassy with the express purpose of studying English architecture, the result was *Das Englische Haus*, published in Berlin in 1904. This book was so influential that English house style became the one to emulate all over northern and central Europe. What appealed so much was the lightness of English interiors, together with the fact that they were functional and made good use of the available space. English house design was taken up with enthusiasm in Europe, so much so that some British architects, notably Charles Rennie Mackintosh, had more success on the Continent than on their native soil. The result was that, with English style as their starting point, Continental architects strode on towards the Modern Movement, while England itself remained locked in the past.

This British conservatism was due to the fact that the features of house style that Muthesius and his compatriots so admired at the beginning of the twentieth century actually had their roots much earlier. These roots were in the English Arts and Crafts Movement started by William Morris in the 1860s, and in the so-called English Domestic Revival or 'Queen Anne' style expounded by Richard Norman Shaw from the 1870s onwards. Both styles harked back in time. Their models were English vernacular architecture, traditional country building that has not been 'designed' but is an organic part of the English countryside. This architecture uses local materials and local skills and its designs are simple and truthful without any attempt to hide the structure of a building with over-ornamentation.

It was to these styles that the speculative Edwardian builder looked for inspiration, despite the fact that by the early years of the twentieth century both the Arts and Crafts Movement and the 'Queen Anne' style had been brought into disrepute. One architect, William Burges, said that the way to design a 'Queen Anne' style building was to 'take an ordinary red brick house and to put [on it] as many gables and dormers and bow windows as possible ... the great object being to get the picturesque by any and every means.' In a similar vein, J. H. Elder-Duncan, writing in *The House Beautiful and Useful* in 1907, described the Arts and Crafts style as 'a desperate endeavour to clothe old articles in new forms, generally with most disastrous results to their practical utility and dubious effect in the matter of abstract beauty'. He continues by saying, 'Their mission seems to be to make complex the already complicated, to make complicated the simple, and to make everything very expensive.'

RIGHT, ABOVE AND BELOW:
Elaborate turned and carved wooden porches, usually painted white, were a regular feature of Edwardian exteriors. In North America, with its long, hot summers, a porch might not only welcome the visitor to the front door, but could also provide a shaded area to sit alongside the house, while in England the function of the porch was more usually simply to shelter the front door.

If the Arts and Crafts Movement and the 'Queen Anne' style provided the artistic details for Edwardian builders, it was the design of the garden cities that influenced the way the new suburbs were laid out. In the mid-nineteenth century philanthropic industrialists in the north of England and the Midlands, influenced by the socialist ideals of thinkers such as William Morris, sought to improve the living conditions of their workforce by providing them with 'model villages' in which to live. The first of these were Copley, Ackroyden and Saltaire, all built between 1849 and 1863. For the first time a village was designed as a unified whole to provide housing for a specific group of people. In London, Bedford Park was started in 1875 under the direction of Norman Shaw, built in the 'Queen Anne' style. It too was designed as an organic whole, but mainly for middle-class artists and writers. The next workers' development was in 1890 at Port Sunlight near Liverpool, built for the Lever Brothers workers. This was followed in 1898 by Bournville for the Cadbury workers and in 1902 by New Earswick for Rowntree workers.

In 1898, Ebenezer Howard set out his ideals for a garden city in *Tomorrow: A Peaceful Path to Real Reform*, and the following year he established the Garden Cities Association. In his book, Howard set out his ideal ratios of people to land and of built-up areas to agricultural land, and he also included provision for transport and for the welfare of the sick and elderly.

Gradually a style developed for garden cities which both nourished and fed upon the speculative building style that was taking root elsewhere. Port Sunlight had its houses arranged in short terraces, each with a different architectural style but all harking back to the vernacular tradition. Lawns in front of the houses, and buildings such as the village pub all added to the sense of community. At Bournville a feature was made of individual gardens, while at Bedford Park, where a number of existing trees had to be preserved and where the site was contained by a railway line and some main roads, the houses could no longer be arranged in formal straight lines as along a typical Victorian street.

Out of Ebenezer Howard's Garden Cities Association there sprang First Garden City Limited, a company of backers that in 1903 bought land at Letchworth in Hertfordshire, north of London. Here the architects Parker and Unwin were able to put into practice the ideals of William Morris and his Arts and Crafts Movement, ensuring that the town plan suited the site's natural features. They decided on a ratio of twelve houses per acre – a ratio that was later to be generally recommended in planning

Once they were no longer associated with housing for the poor, blocks of flats for the middle classes sprang up in British and American town and city centres. The red brick work, white detailing and turreted towers that were so much part of the vernacular revival were adapted to fit city-centre mansion blocks, although these were a far cry from the traditional English country cottages that had originally inspired Richard Norman Shaw and Charles Voysey.

guides – and designed the houses to ensure that the maximum amount of natural light fell in all the rooms, so there were neither the basements nor back extensions typical of Victorian homes. Sometimes the houses at Letchworth had no wall between the front and back rooms on the ground floor. This was a revolutionary idea that did not really take root for many years, but it flew straight in the face of Victorian pretension which held that the rooms for family life had to be kept separate from those for receiving guests.

The garden cities appealed to the Edwardian obsession with fresh air and health. It was as though people wished to throw open the windows of their old, stuffy Victorian homes and introduce some fresh air in the literal as well as the figurative sense. Gordon Allen, writing in 1919 in *The Cheap Cottage and Small House*, echoed Ebenezer Howard: 'The deterioration in the health of town dwellers can be stopped if they be encouraged and assisted to spread themselves over a larger area of land. Everybody then will stand a better chance of obtaining a proper share of sunshine and air.' The Garden City Movement made this possible, showing 'the townsman that he and his family can enjoy a cottage and garden in the country at no more cost than that of the suburban house or town flat.'

For those who did not want to move wholesale to the country, but who wished to enjoy the benefits of larger homes with gardens while retaining the delights that the town had to offer, the garden suburb was the answer. Hampstead Garden Suburb in north London was designed, like Letchworth, by Parker and Unwin. With its houses priced from £425 to £3,500 it was supposed to provide housing for a wide range of people and was to have fostered a true sense of community. Unfortunately it failed in both these aims. The first purchasers of the houses were almost all middle class and, since shops and pubs were not allowed in the development, there was nowhere for the community to come together apart from the church and chapel.

The social engineering intended for Hampstead Garden Suburb may have failed, but the development succeeded in the architectural sense. The appearance if not the reality of a village remains in the intimacy of its short, curving tree-lined streets surrounding a central square. The houses, built in a variety of vernacular styles and ranging from terraced to detached, give the impression of a village that has evolved naturally along narrow country lanes.

Perhaps one of the reasons for the middle-class rush to buy up Hampstead Garden Suburb was the desire for those of modest means to ensure that their neighbours were respectable. Thus a middle-class clerk who could only afford one of the £425 houses could be sure that his neighbours had the same values as himself. *Everywoman's Encyclopaedia* of 1912 carried an article by W.S. Rogers, a civil engineer. Mr Rogers set out not only to educate his readers in how to choose a house that would be draught- and damp-free, but also in how to choose one that would accord with their social status: 'When, owing to the smallness of the household, or slenderness of means, one has to seek a house of moderate rental, a difficulty will be found in regard to the class of people that may be one's neighbours. In towns and suburban districts the street takes its character from that of the majority of

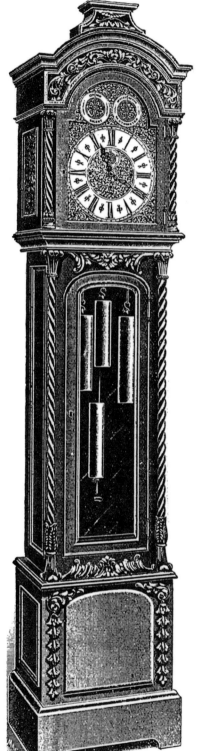

In direct contrast to the over-decorated High Victorian style, the Edwardians preferred cleaner, simpler lines.

AMERICAN & IDEAL
RADIATORS | BOILERS

its occupants, and persons of refined tastes would find it impossible to live up to their usual standard of comfort in a district tenanted by people inspired by a different set of ideals. Amongst the disconcerting factors to be reckoned with are the presence of noisy children in the roadway, street music in generous abundance, hawkers of sturdy lung-power, and disturbances from early risers and late home-comers.' In an environment such as Hampstead Garden Suburb, such inconveniences were unlikely to be a problem. For those with money to spare, finding neighbours of one's own sort was not a problem. The *nouveaux riches* merchants, bankers, brewers and industrialists were now building the sort of homes in the country that the landed classes had built in the eighteenth and nineteenth centuries. While the architects of Edwardian middle-class suburbia were anonymous followers of the trends set by the Arts and Crafts Movement, the architects of the wealthy were men such as Charles Voysey and Edwin Lutyens in England and Charles Rennie Mackintosh in Scotland. These were architects who hoped to set a trend while indulging the whims of their rich masters. Their confections were built in styles ranging from English vernacular through Edwardian Classicism to early Modernism, and for the first

RIGHT: *The granite of Castle Drogo's walls is softened in the drawing room by the elegant wood panelling painted in a soft stippled green. Delicate Venetian chandeliers and comfortable upholstery make this a serene but welcoming room.*

BELOW: *The library together with the adjoining billiard room, make an imposing space. The oak bookcases were designed by Lutyens for the room and were almost the last fittings to be built for the castle.*

years of the twentieth century their designs led the way for the western world.

Voysey was an exponent of the vernacular style. He had been a pupil of Richard Norman Shaw and, like him, appreciated the traditional English architecture of the cottage and manor house. His mainly small, detached houses, finished in rough plaster-work with slate roofs blend perfectly with their natural surroundings. Long and low, often with roofs that project well beyond the walls and rest on slender wrought-iron brackets, the features that made a Voysey house were, according to Nikolaus Pevsner, imitated by 'speculative builders all along the arterial roads and all over the suburbs'.

Lutyens' work consisted mostly of large houses for industrialists and bankers, and culminated in the commission for the city of New Delhi and in particular the Viceroy's House. His work was also very much rooted in the past. His early red-roofed, tile-hung and half-timbered Surrey houses show his love for the simplicity of the English country cottage. Munstead Wood, which he built for Gertrude Jekyll, the garden designer, was described by her as being 'designed and built in the thorough and honest spirit of the good work of old days'.

Inspired by the past, but contrasting dramatically with Munstead Wood, is Lutyens' Castle Drogo, started in 1911 and ready for habitation in 1927. This is a work of sheer bravura. Here Lutyens was working in stone, his favourite material. Drogo stands like a huge granite outcrop lowering over the Devon moorland. Its owner was Julius Drewe, founder of the Home and Colonial Stores and typical of the new wave of

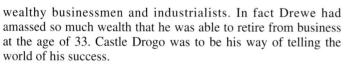

wealthy businessmen and industrialists. In fact Drewe had amassed so much wealth that he was able to retire from business at the age of 33. Castle Drogo was to be his way of telling the world of his success.

Others, perhaps a touch more modest, also had Lutyens design for them, and again the architect drew on the past for his inspiration. Deanery Gardens, built between 1899 and 1902 for Edward Hudson, proprietor of *Country Life* magazine, is a twentieth-century version of an old English manor house. Middlefield, built 1908 near Cambridge and The Salutation, built 1911-12 in Sandwich, Kent, are in a neo-Georgian style which has been copied by twentieth-century architects ever since.

This neo-Classical revival that is now often associated with Lutyens was actually one of a series of revivals that had started

The light and airiness of Edwardian interiors required much less clutter and simpler furniture styles than the highly ornate examples preferred in Victorian times.

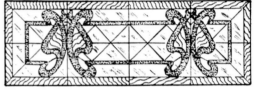

in the late nineteenth century. In France in the 1890s there had been a revival of the Empire style, with the Parisian firm of Jeanselme showing an Empire bedroom at the Paris Exhibition of 1889. The French indulged in decor of this style until well into the 1920s. A parallel revival, this time of the rather severe, unornamented Biedermeier style, was taking place simultaneously in Germany and Austria.

The English neo-Classical look was, nevertheless, very highly prized in Europe. In 1919, only a few months after the Armistice, an English neo-Georgian scheme for a drawing room was reproduced in a German journal. One of the jewels in the crown of Edwardian neo-Classicism must, however, have been John Kinross's transformation of Sir James Miller's eighteenth-century home, Manderston in Berwickshire. Sir James was the son of a very successful merchant, typical of those who, like Julius Drewe had made money and acquired property in the late nineteenth century. Kinross was given a free hand with the refurbishment of the house, and the result, completed in 1905, is a

magnificent combination of eighteenth-century French and English formality with Edwardian comfort and some touches of eccentricity.

While neo-Classicism was giving the public forms it was used to, Art Nouveau was opening its eyes to other possibilities that were to have reverberations throughout Europe and the United States. This colourful style, with its sinuous, three-dimensional forms, posed a real challenge to architects and was only taken up on a limited scale in Belgium, France, Germany and Spain by people like Victor Horta, Henri van de Velde and Antonio Gaudi. In other countries Art Nouveau design was largely confined to wallpaper and small objects such as jewellery, door handles and lamps.

In Scotland, the main exponent of Art Nouveau was Charles Rennie Mackintosh, the leader of the so-called Glasgow School of Art. He started out in the early 1890s designing posters and metalwork in Art Nouveau style. Combining this with a love of Scottish castles and baronial halls he produced work in

the Glasgow area that is both unique and totally modern in its feel. His rectilinear forms are sparse and functional, but many interiors are softened by white paint and his use of subtle curved motifs, often stylized roses and flower buds. In keeping with Arts and Crafts principals, he liked to design all the details of a building, down to the furniture, textiles and metalwork.

In 1901 he was invited to Vienna to decorate and furnish a room for the Secessionist Exhibition. It was a resounding success and was followed by similar successes in Italy and Germany. The Secessionists were so enamoured of Mackintosh that they decorated the pages of their journal *Ver Sacrum* Mackintosh-style. Mackintosh must have been overwhelmed. He had never been so successful at home, nor in England where his only commission had been to remodel a house in Northamptonshire. In 1914 he left Scotland for good.

The Secessionists who had so fallen in love with Mackintosh were a group of sculptors, architects and painters reacting against the stultifying style of the Vienna Academy of Fine Art. In 1897-98 the Secessionists commissioned the Viennese architect Joseph Olbrich to design a boldly beautiful exhibition hall and club-house for them, topped with a romantic open-work dome. Olbrich had been the pupil of Otto Wagner, another Viennese architect who had worked in the neo-Renaissance style. However, in 1894 Wagner was appointed Professor at the Vienna Academy and immediately started to campaign against copying the styles of past ages, thus setting the trend for the Secession school.

In the United States, another architect was busy turning his back on the past. This was Frank Lloyd Wright, a pupil of Louis Sullivan. In 1892 Sullivan had written *Ornament in Architecture*, a manifesto which described ornament as a luxury not a necessity, as something that should be integral to the building itself, not tacked on afterwards. In his revolutionary designs, Frank Lloyd Wright tried to find a style that better expressed the spirit of America than the compartmentalized homes of the nineteenth century. He opened up spaces so that living rooms flowed into dining rooms that flowed into kitchens. Large horizontal expanses of glass brought outdoor spaces indoors, and the outdoors was always present in his use of wood, stone and terracotta. This was what he called 'organic architecture', houses that seemed to grow from their surroundings in the same way that Voysey had intended. Like Voysey, he too insisted on designing all the details of a house – the furniture, textiles, stained-glass windows, lighting, even the panelling to conceal the radiators.

So England had had its effect on the rest of the world. Wagner, Sullivan, Van de Velde and Wright all acknowledged their debt. English style, so beautifully epitomized in Edwardian suburban and garden-city architecture, had been for many the pinnacle of achievement. After World War I, however, the needs of a machine-orientated mass market had to be met, and English architects failed to live up to their earlier promise. The initiative for the Modern Movement or International Style that was to meet these needs was stolen by the Continent and the United States; England was too rooted in its class prejudices to concern itself with the masses, and was the poorer for it.

Chapter 1

The Plan and Façade

'Do not allow your judgement to be influenced by external features.
Builders indulge in flights of fancy in the form of gables, verandahs
and other embellishments designed to please the eye of the
inexperienced. Such features may or may not detract from the
convenience of the house internally, but it is obvious that they
represent value which in many cases would be better spent
inside the house.'

Everywoman's Encyclopaedia, 1912

OPPOSITE PAGE AND BELOW:
The leafy suburbs beckoned the
new middle classes, offering
them a taste of the countryside
within commuting distance of
the city centre. Fresh white
paintwork and verdant gardens
dispelled the severity of the
Georgian terraced house.

By the time of Queen Victoria's death, certain changes were beginning to make their mark on new housing. Over the next twenty years or so the outer suburbs grew steadily to accommodate the ever-increasing number of homeowners, the terraced house became unfashionable, floor plans changed from those of the eighteenth and nineteenth centuries to recognizably modern floor plans, and the demand for flats grew.

Writing at the turn of the century for a German audience, Muthesius remarked that the English leasehold system made it possible for Englishmen 'of every level of income' to live in a private house. He stated that the cost of housing in England was two-thirds the price of that in Germany, while in the suburbs it was half. With housing so affordable there was a rash of house-building in the suburbs and garden cities to meet the demand. Now that there was more space than there had been in over-crowded Victorian city centres, the terraced house, whose basic layout had remained unchanged for 150 years, gradually fell from favour. The uniformity of the terrace never really suited the Victorians with their love of individuality, and it was certainly too rigid a format for the new vernacular styles. For the last quarter of the nineteenth century Victorians had been adding ever more ornament to their terraced homes in an attempt to conceal the fact that they were terraced. Now came the opportunity to build the more desirable suburban villas.

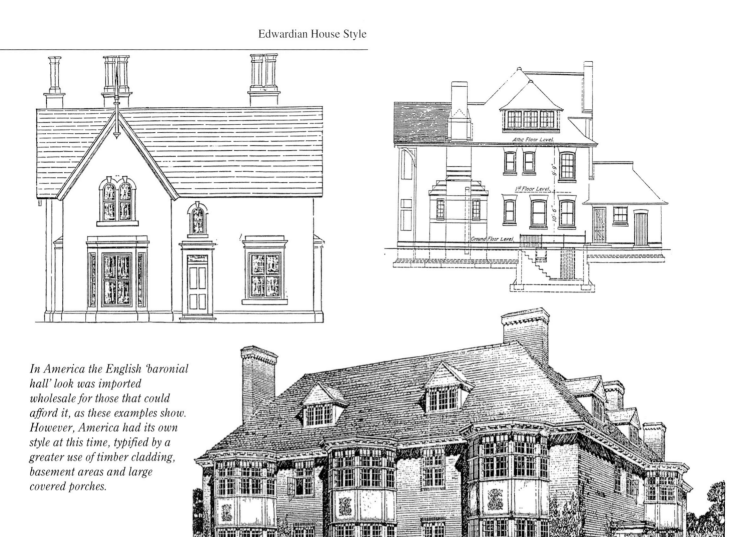

In America the English 'baronial hall' look was imported wholesale for those that could afford it, as these examples show. However, America had its own style at this time, typified by a greater use of timber cladding, basement areas and large covered porches.

There were other reasons, too, why the old, many-storeyed terraced house was no longer fashionable. With their endless stairs and numerous 'domestic offices' – kitchens, sculleries, larders and pantries – they needed an army of servants to run them. However, change was just around the corner. The new labour-saving devices meant that fewer servants were needed. Electric lighting did not need servants to trim the wicks and fill the oil, gas fires did not require the grates to be cleaned and the coals to be carried, and modern plumbing did not need servants to carry water and empty the slops. In addition, fewer people wanted to enter domestic service, despite the fact that, on the whole, the English treated their servants well. In *The House Beautiful and Useful* of 1907, J.H. Elder-Duncan remarked that 'A revolt against the conditions of domestic service has had, and will yet have, a great influence on the furnishing and decoration of our homes.'

The Suburban Villa

So it was inevitable that the layout of homes would change. Smart terraced town homes with a 20-foot frontage and a front block two rooms deep gave way to homes with a 25-foot frontage and deeper site. Now there was scope for an inner hall large enough for entertaining and, instead of the old, single staircase rising from the hall, a separate service staircase meant that the servants could go about their duties without having to cross the hall and interfere with the guests.

The inner suburbs, where space was at a premium, were still characterized by the deadening uniformity of the terrace. The more modest owners of such homes still lived with the division between the front or 'best' room and the rear dining room. In his plans for homes at Letchworth, Unwin tried to do away with the front room, but met with resistance. According to Muthesius, 'nothing in the world would persuade these people to forgo a drawing room such as real "well-to-do" people have'. Other adventurous souls attempting to tinker with the traditional floor plan suggested that houses be built with stairs rising from the living room, thus obviating the need for a hall or passage, but such an idea was abhorrent to a people who so valued their privacy that

OPPOSITE PAGE: *Large bay windows punctuating the façade, and dormers breaking the roof line were a dramatic departure from the flat-fronted late eighteenth and early nineteenth-century terraces, but many Edwardian suburban developments (left and below) possessed a uniformity of their own.*

In town locations narrow frontages with many storeys were still the norm, but in the suburbs and rural areas, two storeys, with the roof space sometimes being used to provide an extra level, were typical. Many of these massive properties survive today, but once cheap servant labour became difficult to find, after the two World Wars, a lot of large houses were demolished to make way for smaller modern properties that were easier to run.

they disliked having the rooms in their homes interconnecting in any way.

There were some variations, however, from the Georgian terrace plan. For a number of years, terraced and other houses were no longer being built with full-sized cellars. Instead, there was often a small cellar beneath the entrance hall into which fuel was tipped through the coal hole in front of the front door. There would also often be a change of level between the front and back blocks of the house, with the rear, slightly lower block housing the kitchen and scullery, and the front block comprising the ubiquitous drawing and dining room. Upstairs were the bedrooms and, with the extra space afforded by the additional rear block, there would also be a bathroom and separate WC, the latter much admired by Muthesius and not often seen on the Continent at that time.

The 20 or 25 foot wide semi-detached house in the new, outer suburbs or garden cities offered more space, but its ground plan remained rather similar to that of the terraced house, whereas a semi-detached house with a frontage of 40 feet had more possibilities. Here, a pleasantly shaped entrance hall could be built, and the kitchen could be farther away from the rest of the house, along a little passageway behind the stairs. The rooms could, of course, be larger and more imposing, in fact more like those of the detached villa to which every Englishman aspired.

It was these detached villas, some for commuters in the outlying suburbs, some weekend homes deeper in the country or homes for those who lived permanently out of town, that were so much admired by England's Continental neighbours. New houses such as these, costing between £1,000 and £5,000, with two to four reception rooms and four to ten bedrooms were regarded as the best that English contemporary architecture could offer. They differed from large country houses only by having a less spacious plan; the number of reception rooms in each would have been roughly the same.

Buying one of the new cheap weekend return tickets issued by the railways, a well-off businessman could now leave his city home for a long weekend in the country. Thanks to the nation's prosperity, England had, by the standards of those times, a short working week. The businessman's weekend home would have greater provision for sitting in the open air than his city home, with a spacious terrace in front of the main rooms and below it a flower garden or lawn. Whereas his city home might still have had a basement, his country home would offer a long, low appearance, with all the domestic offices on the ground floor.

Three or four reception rooms were common: there was always a drawing room and dining room, but if space was limited a choice might have to be made between a billiard room and a library. In the larger home the billiard room was rarely omitted, but the library might be replaced with a morning or breakfast room, and books would go in the hall or dining room. In the smaller home the breakfast room might take precedence over the billiard room or library. According to Muthesius, the English regarded a house with only two reception rooms as having few possibilities 'outside the lower middle class' unless the hall was large enough to use as a reception room.

OPPOSITE PAGE, ABOVE LEFT: *While most of the Edwardian middle classes had to make do with anonymously designed suburban homes, there were those who could aspire to something grander.*

OPPOSITE PAGE, BELOW LEFT: *This house with its 'Queen Anne'-inspired façade might have been one of those Gordon Allen had in mind in the introduction to his* The Cheap Cottage and Small House *(1919). Here he called for an end to houses with ostentatious façades and squalid rear elevations – 'Queen Anne fronts and Mary Ann backs'.*

LEFT: *Architects on the Continent admired the English home for its good use of space. Here a two-storey bay cleverly fills the corner.*

ABOVE: *The combination of a half-timbered effect with overhanging eaves provides an attractive verandah – a feature much loved by the Edwardians.*

THIS PAGE AND OPPOSITE PAGE, BELOW: *This ground-floor plan of a substantial detached house shows many of the features typical of houses of the time. The front door leads into a vestibule which gives onto a square hall with the staircase rising from one corner. Of the three reception rooms, all have window seats and bay windows.*

OPPOSITE PAGE, ABOVE: *The plans for an equivalent American house show a similar arrangement on the ground floor, but this property has a cellar and roofed-over porch, as well as a porch for the servants to sit out.*

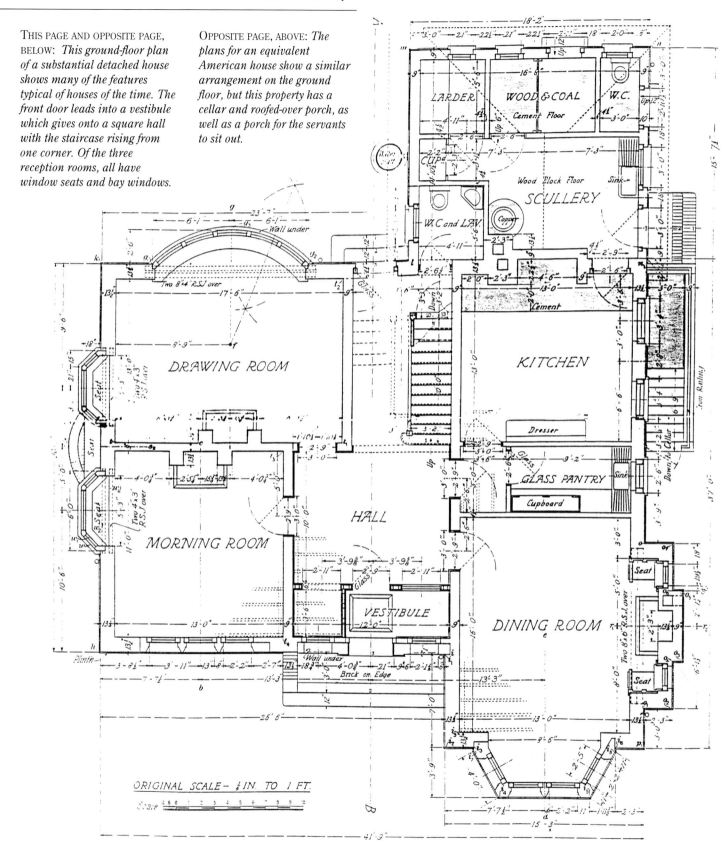

ORIGINAL SCALE – ¼ IN. TO 1 FT.

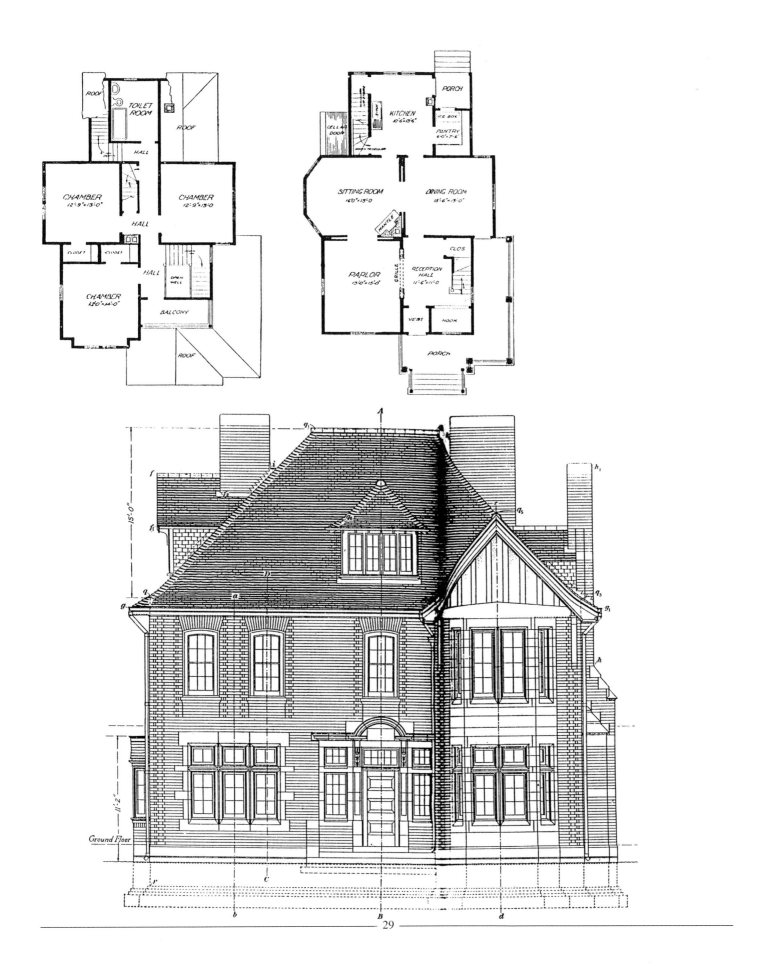

TOILET ROOM

ROOF

ROOF

HALL

CHAMBER
12'-9" x 13'-0"

CHAMBER
12'-9" x 13'-0"

HALL

CLOSET

CLOSET

HALL

OPEN WELL

CHAMBER
18'-0" x 14'-0"

BALCONY

ROOF

PORCH

KITCHEN
10'-6" x 13'-6"

ICE BOX

CELLAR DOOR

PANTRY
6'-0" x 7'-6"

DOWN TO CELLAR

SITTING ROOM
16'-0" x 15'-0"

DINING ROOM
15'-6" x 15'-0"

MANTLE

PARLOR
13'-0" x 15'-0"

GRILLE

RECEPTION HALL
11'-6" x 11'-0"

CLOS

VEST

ROOM

PORCH

15'-0"

11'-2"

Ground Floor

The number of reception rooms was all-important, though with society becoming less formal there were some changes. J. H. Elder-Duncan noted the 'spirit of democracy' that was gradually 'breaking down the barrier of "appearances" and the fiction that the possession of many sitting rooms is a guarantee of respectability'. However, the English, with their keen sense of privacy, liked to have many rooms: modern architects tried to break the mould, but houses with few, decent-sized rooms were hard to find. Developers were, as is often the case, more interested in following the fashion than in setting it.

One of the fashions that was gaining ground, however, was that of living in flats. These had long been popular on the Continent and in Scotland, but they reminded the English too much of hotels. Flats had the advantage, though, of requiring fewer servants and so were becoming popular with people whose main home was in the country, with young married couples, with bachelors and unmarried ladies, and with those who had limited resources but who wanted to live in a nice neighbourhood.

Where space permitted, blocks of flats were built with a large central courtyard, but people still wanted their best rooms to

THIS PAGE: *Pargetting and tile-hanging were two popular methods of weatherproofing and decorating old timber-framed houses. In the mid-1800s architects such as Richard Norman Shaw were incorporating similar features for wealthy clients in their 'Old English' style of architecture. By the 1900s, architects and builders were providing the same for the middle classes everywhere.*

Left and Below: *By the early years of the twentieth century pargeting – the traditional seventeenth-century technique of decorating plaster work with incised lines and embossed patterns – was one of the features of new suburban homes throughout England.*

Now that the parapet walls of early nineteenth-century houses had disappeared, leaving the roof on view, roof coverings played an important part in the decoration of a house. Slate was still used, especially in areas where it was readily available, but many Edwardian homes had roofs made of red tile, obtainable in a large variety of profiles. Tiles were also used as a decorative feature on walls and gable ends, and some attractive fish-scale effects were achieved.

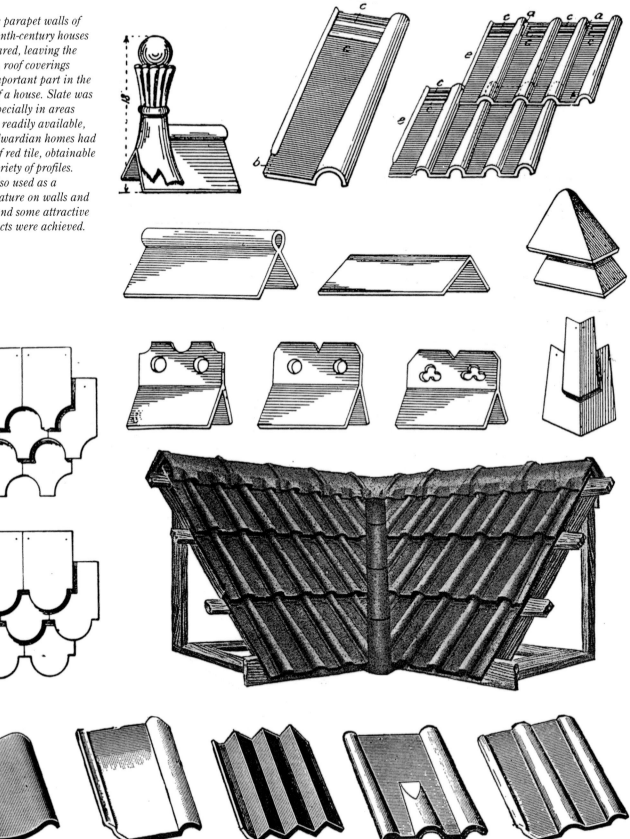

RIGHT: *In the* Architectural Record *of September 1915, the American Herbert Croly recorded that 'The reaction against building palaces has won a complete triumph, and the good American, no matter how wealthy he may be, is now content to live in a comparatively modest and unpretentious house.' This house, built around that time on the west coast of America, seems to have escaped that general trend. It is, however, a glorious example of how the vernacular revival crossed the Atlantic.*

OPPOSITE PAGE, ABOVE LEFT*: A fine pair of double doors and sunray canopy are attractive features of this suburban house.*

OPPOSITE PAGE, BELOW LEFT: *Edwardian architects took advantage of the spaciousness of the new suburbs to build houses with wider frontages and projecting bay windows to make up for the lost basement areas.*

OPPOSITE PAGE, BELOW RIGHT: *In the suburbs, even a terraced house could afford to have many spacious, well-lit rooms.*

overlook the front of the block rather than the courtyard. Back stairs were not popular because it was impossible to keep a check on who might be trying to gain access, so a lift took goods up from the courtyard to the various floors. Just as in houses, interconnecting rooms were not popular, so every flat had its hallway with the separate rooms leading off it. However, the feeling that one might be in a hotel was reinforced by the style of the block's main entrance hall. This was always large and well-appointed, often with wood panelling and a fireplace, and there was always a lift.

The Vernacular Revival

Externally, too, homes were undergoing a great change. The fashion for the revived vernacular styles led to there no longer being a proper distinction between structure and ornament. Features such as pargetting, tile-hanging, roughcast walls and half-timbering made a come-back, but whereas these features had once been a structural necessity, in Edwardian hands they became mere decoration.

The vernacular revivals demanded that local building materials be used. Better transport had widened the range of materials available to builders, but time and again, the arbiters of taste argued for local materials to be used on both aesthetic and economic grounds. In *The House We Ought to Live In* (1923), John Gloag even goes so far as to show a five-bedroomed house in concrete for an urban location, in brick and tile for a south-eastern location and in stone for the Cotswolds and the West Country.

THIS PAGE: *Gable ends, bargeboards and roof finials were often decorated with very attractive wood carving as in these American examples.*

OPPOSITE PAGE LEFT: *A variety of decorative window frames were used to let light into gable rooms.*

OPPOSITE PAGE RIGHT: *The problem of ensuring adequate ventilation in the roof space was often dealt with by means of an amusing-looking ventilator of the type shown here. They were available in all shapes and sizes, from Chinese pagoda, to dovecote, to medieval turret.*

Wood-turning reached its peak of perfection on the exterior of the Edwardian suburban villa. Fantastic examples abound, ranging from Gothic-style canopies and porches (ABOVE AND RIGHT)*, delicate verandahs with a Regency feel like this North American example* (TOP)*, and elaborate fretwork recalling the carved marble of Moorish Spain and North Africa* (OPPOSITE PAGE)*.*

The clock could not be turned back, though. People wanted to benefit from being able to build a stone house in Kent, or one with fake half-timbering in a north London suburb, in the same way as they wanted to benefit from the cheapness of the new cavity walls and concrete. Any material was possible anywhere in the country. In *The Cheap Cottage and Small House* (1919), Gordon Allen was able to describe garden village cottages in Crayford in Kent built from concrete with tiled roofs and roughcast rendering, a cottage near Horsham in Surrey made with cavity walls, whitewashed and tile-hung, a house in Hampstead, north London of bricks and roughcast with a tiled roof, and a cottage at Walgrave, Northamptonshire of the same materials.

As demanded by the vernacular taste, roofs in red tile or slate were tall and sweeping, sometimes punctuated by fairytale turrets and often ending in generous gables outlined with white-painted bargeboards. There were many chimneys, for the English still loved open fires, but stylish new homes had their chimneys grouped in one or two large central stacks which were not only better to look at, but more economic to build.

As this advertisement for 'a thoughtfully constructed chimney pot' shows, down draughts, causing smoke from an open fire to be forced back into the room, were a constant preoccupation of the Edwardians. With heating by stove more prevalent on the Continent, Hermann Muthesius writing in Das Englische Haus was amazed that, with all their other domestic conveniences, the English were prepared to put up with open fires, smoky chimneys and draughty rooms.

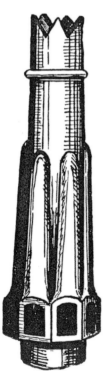

The Edwardian Chimney Pot

NATIONAL SCHEME FOR DISABLED MEN

Telephone No.:
Victoria 5846.
Telegrams:
'Abednego, Sowest, London."

Frustrating Downdraught

A thoughtfully constructed chimney pot successfully designed to put a stop to the ever prevalent discomfort of smoky rooms.

Even chimneystacks might be decorated with elaborate brickwork, moulded terracotta panels and castellations.

No longer the narrow, panelled front door with fanlight above of the Georgian or early Victorian home, the Edwardian front door announced its individuality with panache. It might be set to one side beneath a tiled overhanging roof (ABOVE), or sheltered by an imposing porch (RIGHT, ABOVE AND BELOW). *It could project* from the side of the house in imitation of a monastic cloister (OPPOSITE PAGE, ABOVE LEFT), *or could face you fair and square* (OPPOSITE PAGE, BELOW LEFT). *Alternatively, it could hide away shyly and let the pilastered canopy take all the glory* (OPPOSITE, RIGHT).

Walls were somewhat disfigured by pipes thanks to a regulation of 1891 stipulating that all waste pipes must be on the outside of a house. Muthesius deplored the resulting 'heedless exposure of supply pipes and drain pipes', but breathed a sigh of relief that the cold climate of England would make this less of a problem than it would be in Germany.

Narrow Victorian front doors were replaced by imposing panelled and glazed doors, often flanked by stained-glass windows. Doors were sometimes painted a vivid red or green, and in summer a linen curtain might shade the front door and hall. For homes in the outer suburbs and in the country a low, wide, solid-looking door was preferred, simply panelled and either stained and polished, or painted and varnished.

To add to the imposing effect and to protect from the elements, the suburban front door was often sheltered by an elaborate canopy of turned spindles and fretwork – a pastiche of country woodworking skills – or by an even more elaborate porch. Set against the red brick walls, the white-painted wood-work of these porches appeared freshly welcoming. In many

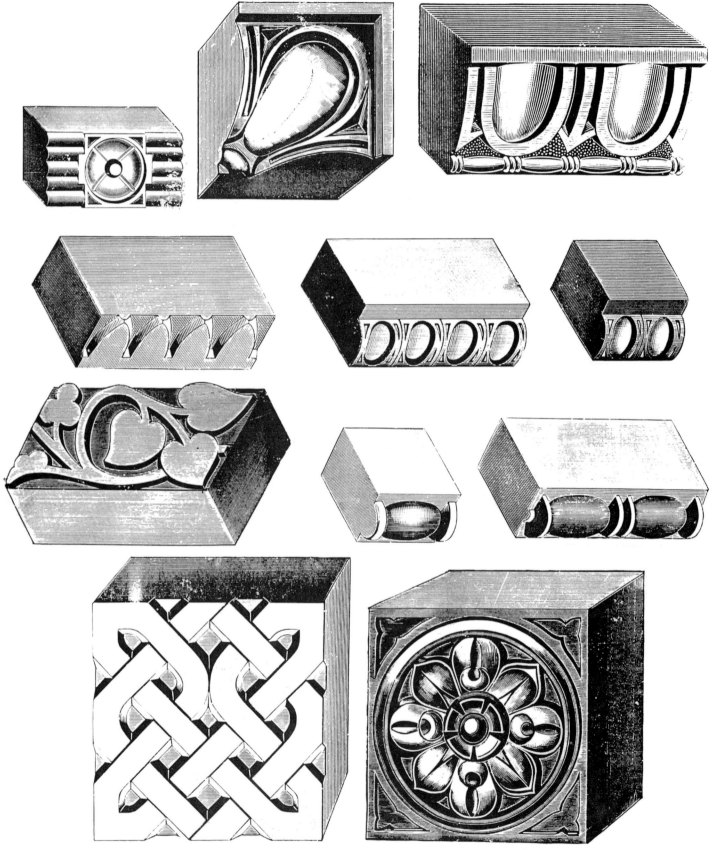

Town dwellers were particularly fond of ornamenting their red-brick houses with terracotta details like these. Such designs were readily available from builders' merchants and might be used as a frieze running under the eaves, to highlight decorative arches, as features beneath windows, or simply as ornaments in their own right.

cases the roof of the house dipped right down to make a porch, or the porch was carried up through two storeys to the main eaves. As an alternative, the front wall of the house might have an arched brick opening containing the porch.

As basements became less common, so there was no need for steps leading up to front doors. The front doorstep which in Victorian England was whitened daily by a maid, was now sometimes covered by a sheet of metal to minimize cleaning. In the suburbs and country a path of stone flags leading to the front door was seen as practical and delightfully 'olde-worlde'.

Door furniture became simpler. Black finishes were more popular than labour-intensive brass and although doorbells had generally come into use, there were still door knockers to be seen everywhere. House numbers in brass were often replaced

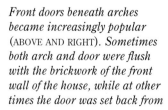

Front doors beneath arches became increasingly popular (ABOVE AND RIGHT). *Sometimes both arch and door were flush with the brickwork of the front wall of the house, while at other times the door was set back from* *the arch to create a porch. Semi-detached and terraced houses might have matched pairs of adjoining front doors* (OPPOSITE PAGE, RIGHT)*, while occasionally a single door appeared to be a pair* (OPPOSITE PAGE, LEFT)*.*

The fashion for roof crests in iron or terracotta had grown since the end of the nineteenth century and continued in Edwardian times as these examples show. The strips were used to decorate a roof ridge and were punctuated at their end – usually above the gable – with a twisted, ball-shaped or acanthus-leaf finial.

The standard four or six-panelled Georgian front door gave way to doors with a multitude of small wood or stained glass panels and plain, arched or ogee-shaped glazing bars.

by enamelled black on white plates or simply by numerals painted on the fanlight above the door.

Window styles were very varied. Despite the problems associated with them, sash windows were still used. Rooms were now lit not by one tall sash window, but by a row of two or three shorter ones, divided from each other by plain wooden jambs or Grecian-style pilasters. The late-Victorian fashion for large panes of glass had passed and an upper, fixed window light was now often subdivided by a tracery of small rectangles, diamonds or lozenge shapes, all picked out in crisp white.

In the most up-to-date homes, built in the 'cottagey' style of Lutyens or Voysey, long rows of low casement windows were used with leaded panes. The windows were separated from each other by wooden, square-section jambs and these were often turned through an angle of 90 degrees for a 'quaint' effect. The wood was either left plain or painted green or brown.

With the revival of Georgian-style architecture, the tall sash window once more prevailed, but the Edwardians departed from the uniformity of Georgian facades by breaking their neo-Georgian facades up with circular, semi-circular and oval windows.

Muthesius commented on the fact that, because there was little sunshine in England, people had no need for verandahs or

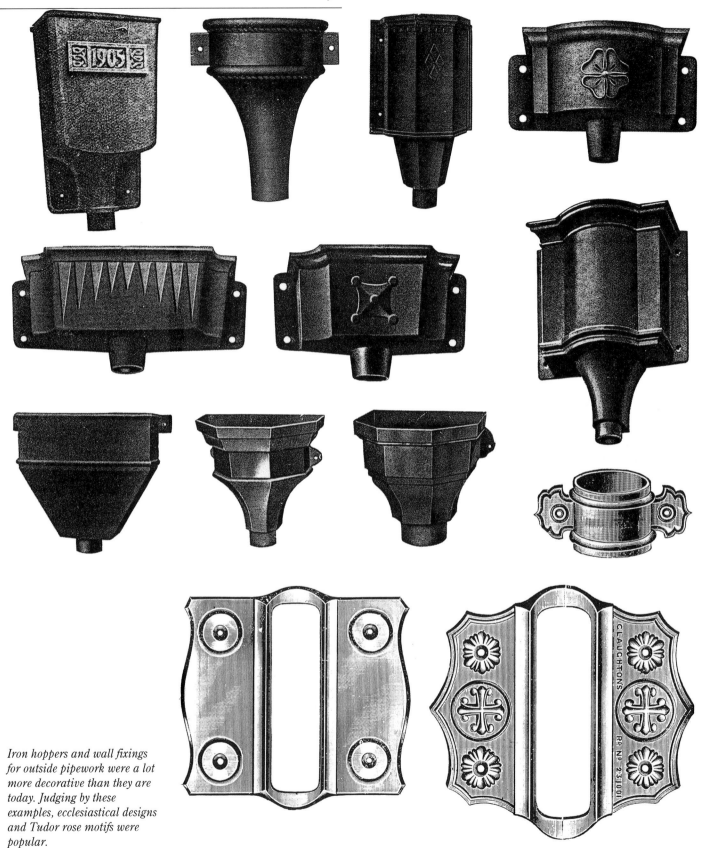

Iron hoppers and wall fixings for outside pipework were a lot more decorative than they are today. Judging by these examples, ecclesiastical designs and Tudor rose motifs were popular.

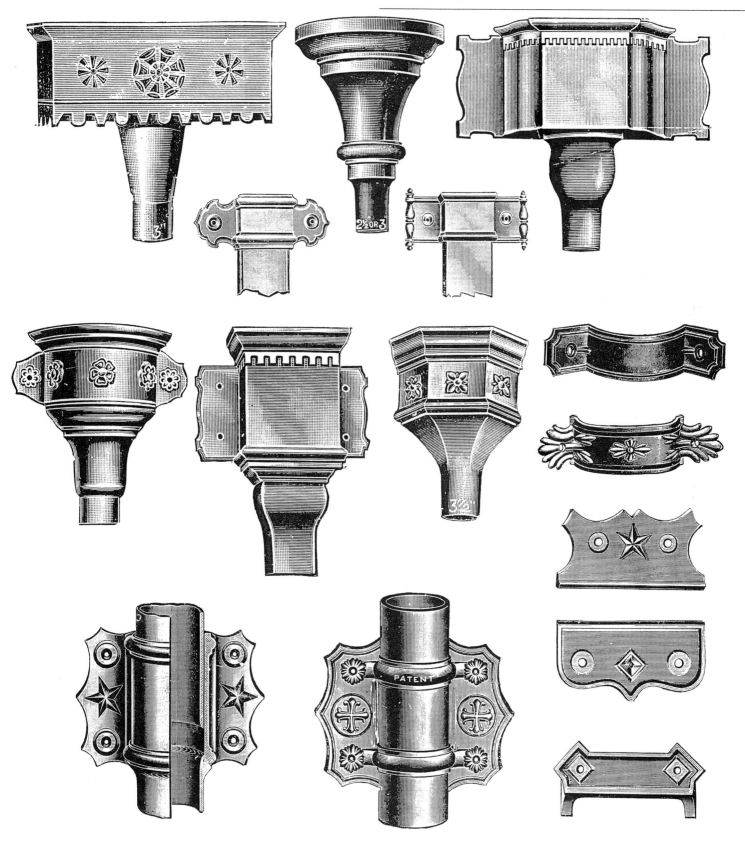

loggias. Bay windows were a popular solution, providing the advantages of an open-air balcony with the shelter of a room. However, the Edwardian fetish for fresh air soon overcame the vagaries of the weather, and once architects like Lutyens had started providing their rich clients with balconies, loggias and open-air sleeping-rooms, it was not surprising that the less wealthy members of the middle class soon demanded the same.

Stained glass gave an ecclesiastical feel that was in keeping with the vernacular revival. The rich colours and dense patterns of Victorian stained glass were gradually eschewed in favour of paler colours and a mixture of stained and etched glass to lighten the effect. The fashion for giving houses names continued from the nineteenth century, and these names were often picked out in stained glass on the fanlight.

These letter boxes, doorbells, knockers and door handles are mostly in the traditional classical styles that were popular in the nineteenth century and that continue to be popular today, but one or two show the influence of Art Nouveau and the Arts and Crafts Movement. Pieces in this latter style are especially suited to cast iron rather than brass and, as servants to polish the brass became harder to come by, many people preferred black door furniture.

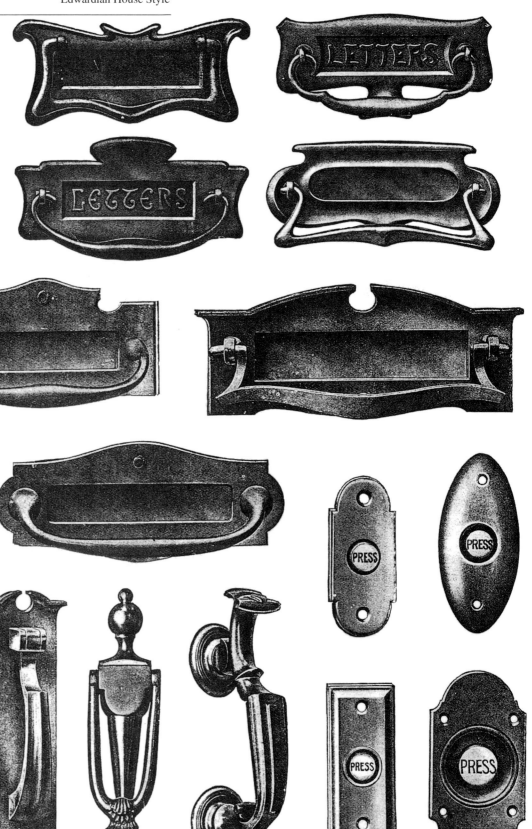

Coloured, glazed tiles were often used for external decoration, particularly on the walls of porches. Some designs were influenced by Art Nouveau (OPPOSITE PAGE, CENTRE) or later by the neo-Georgian revival.

Front paths inlaid with encaustic tiles continued to be popular well into the twentieth century but Edwardian colouring was less strident than that of the Victorians, with black, white, grey, beige and terracotta predominating. Fussy Victorian floral designs with elaborate panels and borders also gave way to simpler geometric motifs.

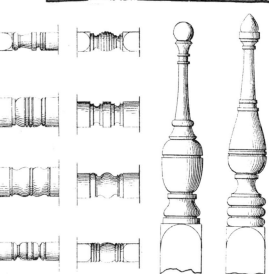

As wood-turning became more sophisticated, so masters of the art could display their talents all over the façade of the Edwardian home – in porches, verandahs and conservatories.

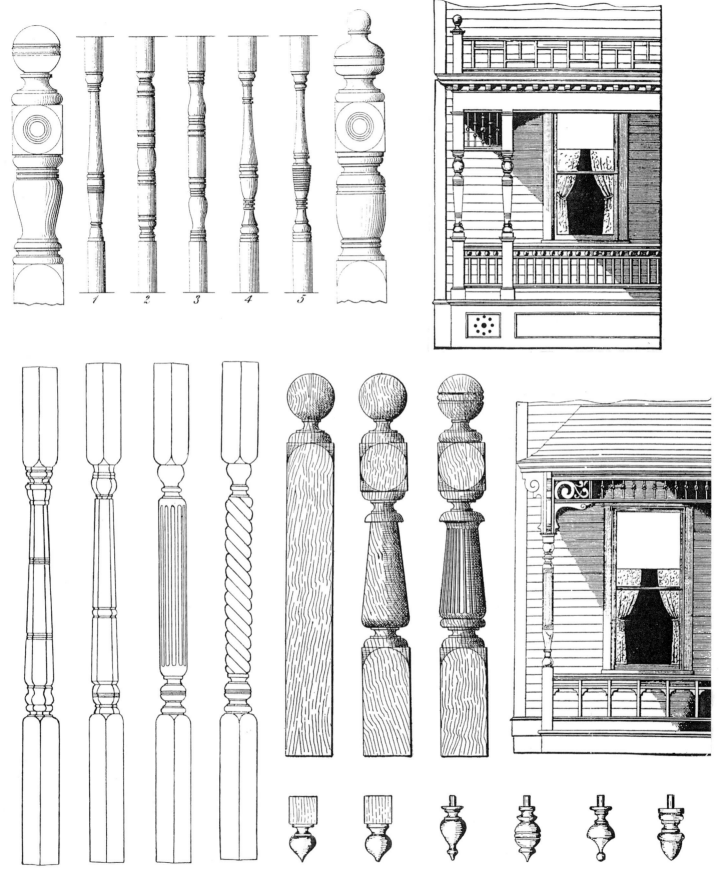

Decorated plaster and terracotta panels were frequently set into the brickwork to enliven a house's exterior. Plants and flowers were a common motif. The owner of the house below shows a sense of humour in positioning a real pot plant on the shelf above the plaster one.

Classical and grotesque faces, even a scene showing sea, plant and bird life – all these were material for the imaginative though often anonymous Edwardian architect.

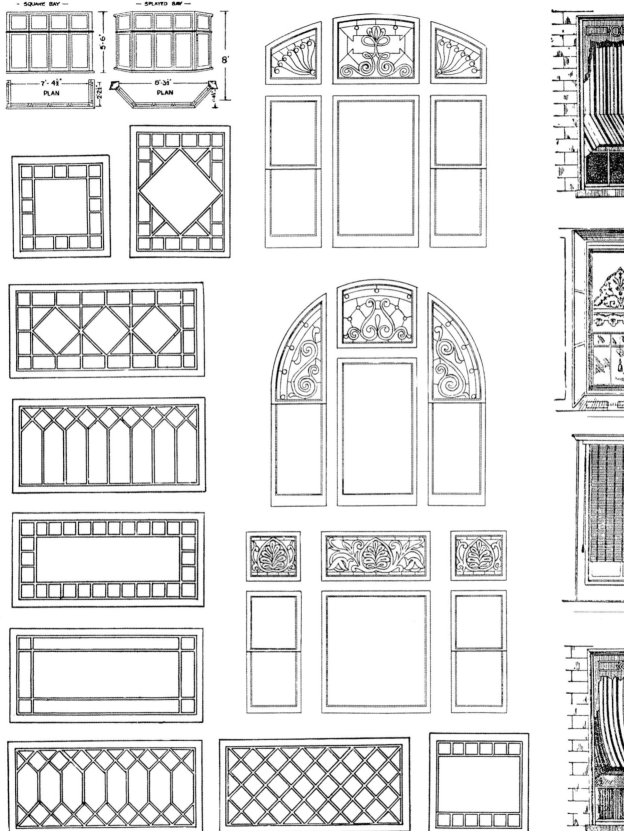

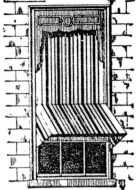

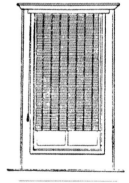

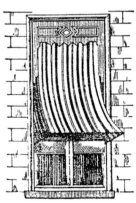

As this selection of windows from turn-of-the-century catalogues shows, the Edwardians had come a long way from the plain sash windows of the Georgians and Victorians. Here, fixed windows rub shoulders with casements fitted into bays, and glazing bars and stained glass provide an assortment of geometric and naturalistic forms. For sunny climates there are some ingenious window blinds.

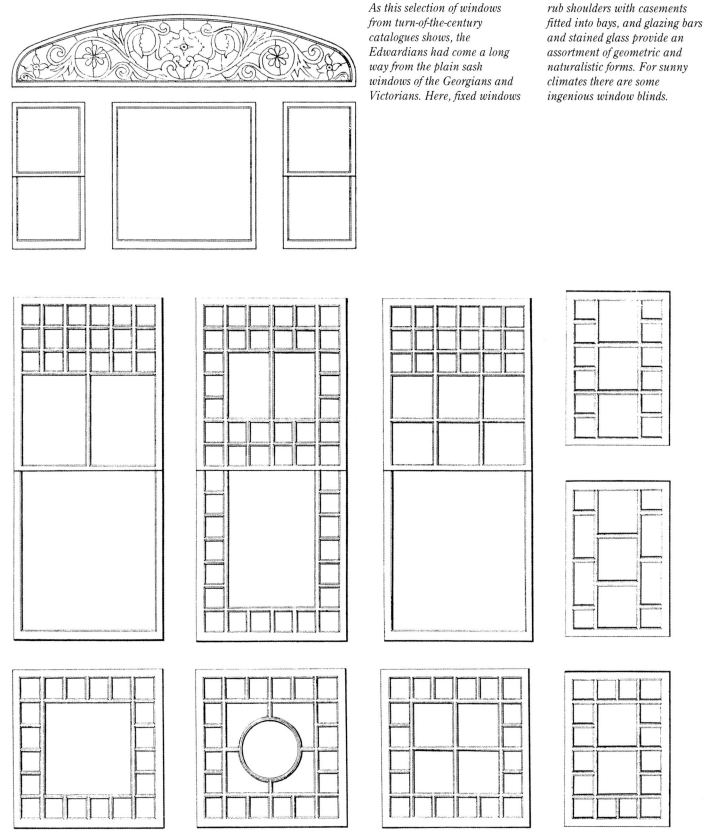

The Edwardians borrowed from many architectural styles.

ABOVE *Fruit-filled terracotta urns mirrored in the owner's amusing windowboxes underline the delicate pattern of glazing bars in this pair of windows.*

ABOVE RIGHT: *A bold red-brick double arch in Norman style frames and links an attractive pair of windows.*

RIGHT: *A Gothic arch forms the focal point of this bay window.*

LEFT: *A brickwork arch softens and frames a large window and emphasizes its delicate stained-glass flower design.*

BELOW: *White-painted pilasters and frieze tie together a group of three sash windows in this striking bay.*

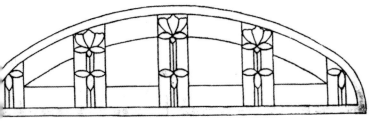

Stained glass included heraldic motifs, neo-Georgian swags, elongated Art Nouveau plant forms and some designs which might have come straight from ancient Egyptian representations of the papyrus and lotus flowers.

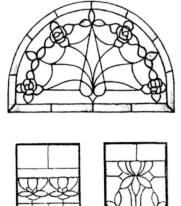

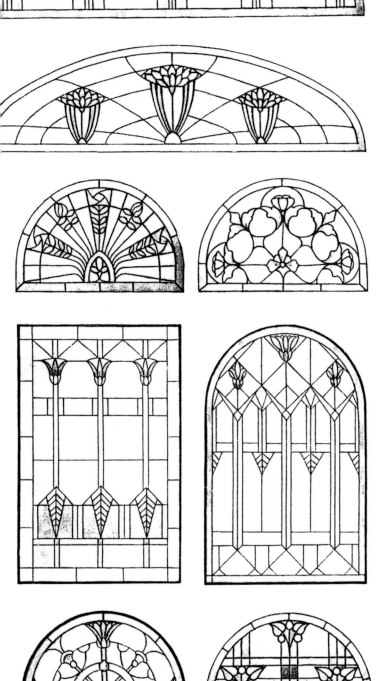

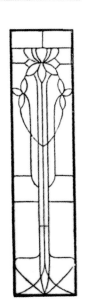

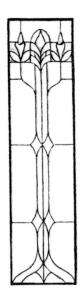

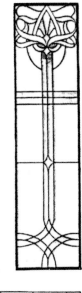

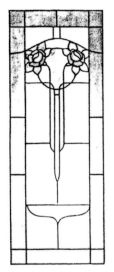

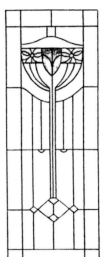

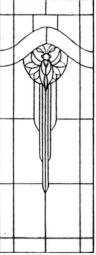

Decorated gable ends were another feature of the English vernacular style that were much loved by the Edwardians. A filling of half-timbering (BELOW) *or a coating of white-painted roughcast* (RIGHT) *gave a real* rus in urbe *feel.*

This elaborate stepped gable end from North America (LEFT, ABOVE) *features decorated bargeboards, a turned-wood balconette and scroll brackets supporting wooden spindles in a sunray pattern. The sunray pattern and decorated bargeboards make another appearance in North America* (LEFT, BELOW).

ABOVE: *An unusual fish-scale effect is achieved in the tile-hung filling to this gable end.*

Wrought-iron continued in popularity for railings, balustrades, porches and verandahs, but as carpentry became more mechanized and as the 'quaint' or 'rustic' look became fashionable, so the demand grew for such items to be made from wood. These examples from builders' catalogues are quite plain compared with some. They might be used outside on a porch or verandah, or inside as part of an arch spanning the hallway.

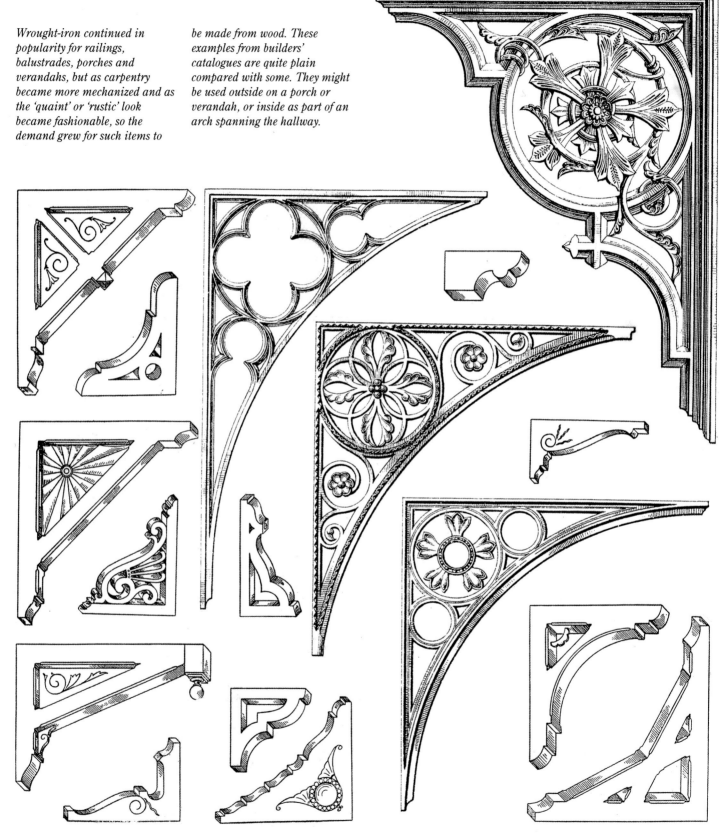

ABOVE: *Terracotta ridge tiles and a group of four chimneypots top the roof of a gable-ended projection.*

RIGHT, BELOW: *This chimneystack with its bricks set at angles might have come from an Elizabethan manor house.*

RIGHT, ABOVE: *This unusual chimneystack is on a house designed by Charles Voysey.*

A pair of elegant wrought-iron
gates forms the perfect foil to the
tiled path and striking front door
of a substantial Edwardian villa.
The uniformity of Georgian
railings and the heaviness of
much of the Victorian wrought-
iron work was now often
superseded by fences and railings
in lighter, sinuous and more
open design.

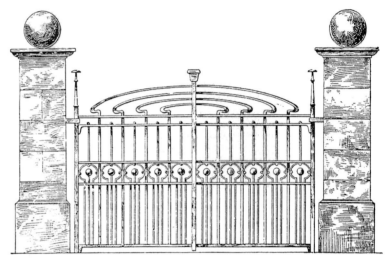

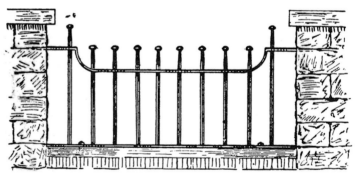

Wrought-iron railings, gates and balconies were common features of Edwardian homes just as they had been in the previous two centuries. Designs varied from the rather severe and classical, that were good accompaniments to neo-Georgian architecture, to the more ornate that suited architecture in the vernacular revival styles. Very large detached houses might have gates and railings boasting armorial devices.

Wrought-iron balconies and balconettes had already featured on private houses for over a hundred years, but in Edwardian times they became larger. Now they might run beneath several windows or might emphasize the shape of a projecting bay beneath while providing an area for sitting out in the sun.

LEFT: *Double wrought-iron gates proclaim the wealth of the middle-class owner of this magnificent detached suburban house. Such a house, like the home of a landed country gentleman, needed an army of domestic servants to run it. At the turn of the century a household costing £1,000 a year required a living-in cook, housemaid, under-housemaid and manservant as well as one or two nannies for the children. Even a household costing £200 a year had one living-in servant.*

ABOVE: *The gilded wrought-iron railings leading to the front door at a smart London address recall the severe austerity of the eighteenth century. They are well suited to the neo-Georgian style of architecture of this house.*

Influenced by the designs of architects such as Charles Voysey, wooden gates like these provided the perfect finish to the boundary of a house in the vernacular style. They formed the ideal complement to a sweeping tiled roof, roughcast walls and strips of leaded casement windows.

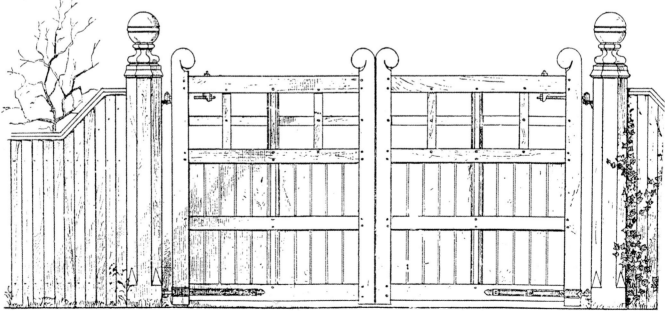

Chapter 2

Hallways and Reception Rooms

'I demand only of a hall that it strikes a note of warmth, of welcome, to the incoming guest. It is really the keynote of the house, and the first impression it makes on you, good or bad, remains, no matter how charming (or the reverse) the rest of the house may be.'

Helen Mathers, 'Colour Sense in Furnishing', *Everywoman's Encyclopaedia*, 1912

OPPOSITE AND BELOW: *Light and airy hallways were a major feature of Edwardian houses, in distinct contrast to those of the Victorian era.*

One of the most dramatic decorative changes to affect the house during the period 1900 to 1920 was the growing popularity of the sitting or living-hall. These had started to become fashionable at the end of the nineteenth century when the Arts and Crafts Movement called for less formality and a return to simplicity and homely rustic values. The hall was to be a place of welcome, where the weary traveller could shed his outdoor clothes, warm his hands by the fire, be greeted by his children and his dog, and sit awhile to relax and perhaps have a warming drink.

A Place of Welcome

New houses in the suburbs and garden cities had wider frontages, so there was often the space for a large hallway. Even a hallway as narrow as five feet would be expected to include a welcoming fireplace, but a square or 'sitting-hall' was best of all and, if screened from the draughts of the front door by some sort of vestibule, it made a charming introduction to the rooms beyond.

In 'The Comforts of a Hall Sitting-Room', *Everywoman's Encyclopaedia* goes to some pains to give the plans of a sitting-hall 'tucked away snugly in the heart of the dwelling' (real Arts and Crafts emotion). It is approached via a glazed porch and then through a small vestibule with double doors flanked by glazed panels. A staircase rises from one corner of the hall, the drawing room leads off on the left and kitchen and dining room on the right. Double doors lead out to the garden and alongside these an imposing bay window juts out beside a verandah. The bay has a cushioned window seat to look out across the garden in summer, while on winter evenings a heavy plush curtain could be drawn across for added cosiness.

Sometimes sitting-halls would even incorporate a dining recess with a wooden banquette round two or three sides of the table. J. H. Elder-Duncan had obviously seen this in what he called an 'advanced art', or Aesthetic home. He did not approve, and wrote with unintended humour that 'these fixed arrangements must be very awkward: for slim, aesthetic people they may answer, for stout people they must be very troublesome'.

The curious aspect of the large sitting-hall is the strange mixture of social values it embodies. On the one hand it represents the homely, 'cottagey', vernacular tradition, but on the other it harks back to the days of the grand baronial hall or the noble entrance halls of the eighteenth century. *Everywoman's Encyclopaedia* waxes lyrical over one of these, the London home of the first Duke of Marlborough with its magnificent old oak staircase, huge oak double doors and welcoming fireplace, grandfather clock and comfortable chairs.Large town houses like this would have the space for all the bits and pieces necessary

for linking the comfortable interior with the less predictable outside world. There would be a cupboard containing a small roll of red carpet for the footman or butler to lay over the pavement when the master or mistress was entering or leaving, an umbrella to protect them from the rain, and a place to keep whistles for summoning a cab or the police.

Furnishing the average Edwardian sitting-hall was, of course, a less grand affair, but the effect was all-important. If you had a fireplace – and one made from rustic-look briquettes was best –

Fretwork had long been popular as a simple craft for making toys and photograph frames. The Edwardians elevated it to the realms of pure fantasy as in this Moorish hall . Fretwork panels similar to these were bought from catalogues and installed in halls as far afield as South Africa and Australia. With Jacobean style very much in vogue, balusters were mass produced in a huge variety of plain turned, turned and twisted, and 'shaped' forms. The Edwardian householder could choose from deal, pitch pine, oak, mahogany or walnut. Only the most avant-garde home would include the absolutely plain, square-section, close-set balusters favoured by designers like Voysey.

THIS PAGE: *These encaustic tiles from an Edwardian builders' catalogue show the variety of patterns that were available. Reproductions of tiles like these can be obtained, or originals can sometimes be found in salvage yards.*

BELOW, RIGHT: *Voysey used unvarnished and unpainted wood to emphasize the homely rustic qualities of the houses he designed.*

OPPOSITE PAGE: *Edwardian hallways frequently had a welcoming open fire. The owner of this house is lucky enough to have the original fireplace with its mahogany surround and stone hearth.*

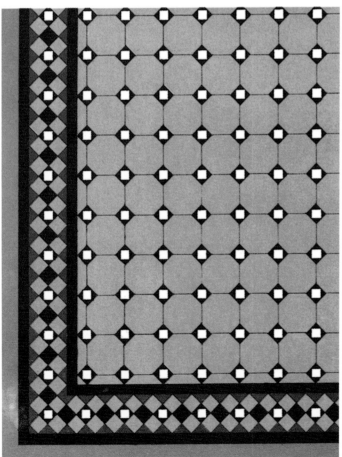

then it was important to make it into an inglenook, with an archway dividing it from the rest of the hall and a fireside settle on either side. Owners of smaller halls had to take great care to keep their furnishings and decoration simple. In 1918, in *Inside the House of Good Taste*, the American Richardson Wright felt that the decoration of a long, narrow 'rat-hole' of a passage 'presents serious difficulties that only heroic treatment can overcome satisfactorily', and he made the revolutionary suggestion of removing the wall between the hall and the living room to provide more space.

An acceptable minimum of furniture would include a chair and hallstand, but with a sitting-hall people thought it best to keep hats and coats out of sight. The hall floor was of wood, tile, concrete or stone, covered with rugs or runners for easy cleaning. In small halls neutral colour schemes were recommended, especially in flats, to avoid a clash of colours when doors leading off the hall would invariably be open.

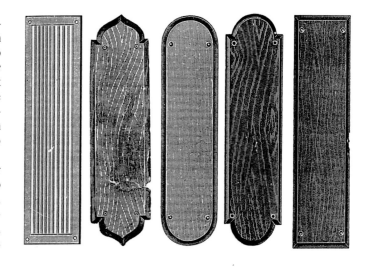

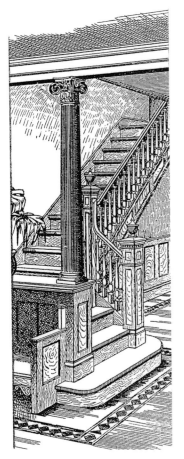

OPPOSITE, ABOVE: *Finger plates were often made of wood.*

OPPOSITE, BELOW: *Although architects like Voysey used the simplest, square-sectioned newel posts, many preferred classical designs with reeding and decorative, urn-shaped finials.*

THIS PAGE: *Elaborate Corinthian columns supporting hall ceilings and screens lent an impression of opulence to many Edwardian hallways, especially in North America. The hallway might even incorporate a 'library corner'.*

BELOW: *The wide front door with extra panel of stained glass and the tiled floor were typical of hallways at the turn of the century. The wall has been divided into dado, filling and frieze, with the frieze delineated by a narrow picture rail.*

RIGHT: *This stunning hall retains the original fretwork screen and balusters. Wider hallways gave the Edwardians the chance to have an imposing staircase with a 90-degree turn like this one.*

OPPOSITE PAGE, ABOVE: *A filigree arch of turned and carved wood spans the hallway of a house in North America.*

OPPOSITE PAGE, BELOW: *The owner of this house has chosen an effective red-tiled flooring to accentuate the colours of the hall's stained glass. Stylized flower motifs such as these owe a great deal to the influence of Charles Voysey.*

Hall walls were either panelled with wood or, if this was too expensive, dark-toned Lincrusta – an embossed wallpaper – was a popular alternative. Exposed black oak ceiling beams suited the sitting-hall, but cheaper stained wood was an acceptable substitute.

Halls were invariably crammed full of knick-knacks and pictures, despite the modern trend for simplicity. Our old friend J.H. Elder-Duncan was very certain on this point: 'Make a clean sweep of antlers, spears, assegais, shields and all the other miscellaneous animal relics and weapons of warfare.' He and others recommended decorating the walls with simple Japanese prints, etchings and sporting prints.

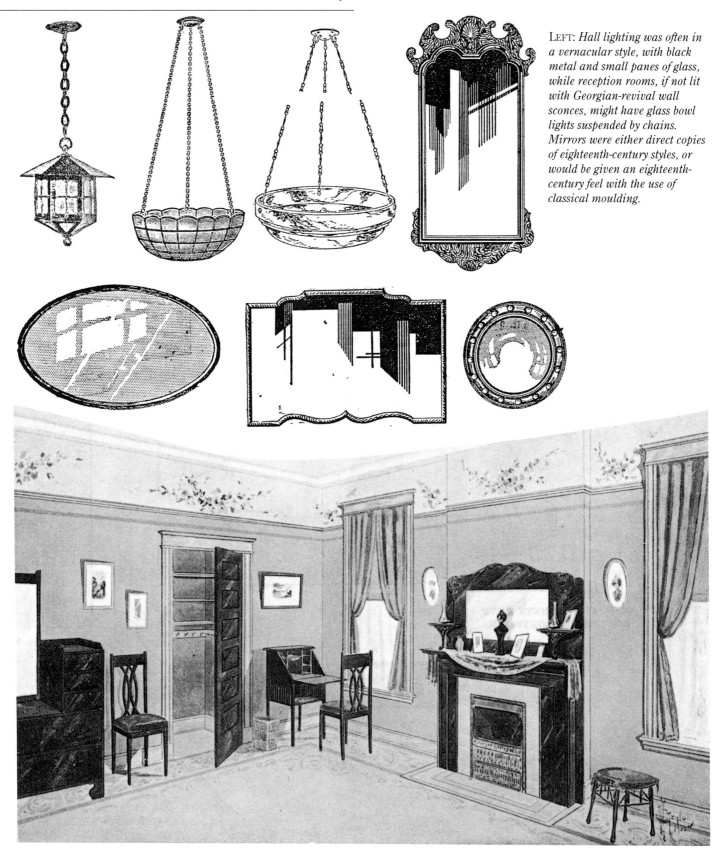

LEFT: *Hall lighting was often in a vernacular style, with black metal and small panes of glass, while reception rooms, if not lit with Georgian-revival wall sconces, might have glass bowl lights suspended by chains. Mirrors were either direct copies of eighteenth-century styles, or would be given an eighteenth-century feel with the use of classical moulding.*

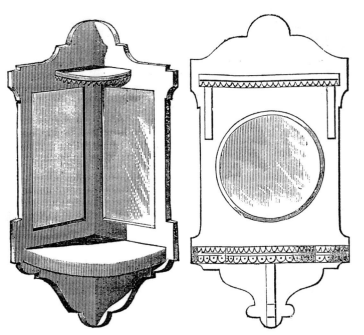

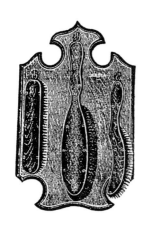

LEFT: *A hallway would often have a small wall mirror, sometimes incorporating a pair of clothes brushes, or the brushes might come as a separate set.*

BELOW: *This panelled dining room has wallpaper in the panels of the dado, a stencilled frieze above, and a ceiling with exposed beams.*

Living Rooms

Having navigated one's way through the perilous waters of the hallway, more dangers lay in wait in the reception rooms. For the late Victorians and early Edwardians, reception rooms were the part of the home that told the outside world who you were and what you were worth. The more reception rooms a person could boast, the higher his standing. For the very wealthy, reception rooms might even include ceremonial rooms such as ballrooms, but on both sides of the Atlantic even the wealthiest were looking for greater simplicity. In *The Decoration of Houses*, published in New York in 1897 and in London in 1898, Edith Wharton and Ogden Codman wrote of the difficulties people were having in trying to combine family and ceremonial use in one room. The results were dismal: 'Nothing can be more cheerless than the state of a handful of people sitting after dinner in an immense ballroom, with gilded ceiling, bare floors and a few pieces of monumental furniture ranged round the walls. A gala room is never meant to be seen except when crowded: the crowd takes the place of the furniture'.

In more modest homes people slowly realized the folly of having 'best' drawing rooms which stood unused for most of the time, and the drawing room gradually gave way to the less formal living room of today. One reason for this was the

OPPOSITE PAGE, ABOVE:
Substantial French windows like these often led out onto a terrace or, in houses with a lower rear block, to a small flight of steps down to the garden.

OPPOSITE PAGE, BELOW:
Matching suites of furniture became popular for living and dining rooms. This ebonized 'bergere' suite with matching china cabinet, bureau, mirror and coffee table epitomizes the then-fashionable taste for 'chinoiserie'. The carpet here is much plainer than would have been the case thirty years before.

THIS PAGE: *An original tiled grate with carved wooden mantelpiece shows that this living room might come from an Edwardian house. Like many other rooms of its time, it would have been decorated with furniture, pictures and china of the eighteenth and nineteenth centuries as well as of the twentieth.*

changing social status of women. As more women were freed from the shackles of formal society life and as ever-increasing numbers took up employment outside the house, they no longer needed a room in which to take tea or do their needlework.

In keeping with these changes in structure, came changes in furniture. The early years of the century still saw plenty of heavy, dark, uncomfortable Victorian furniture, but this slowly gave way to furniture that was lighter in colour and style. Suites of furniture started to be made, and companies such as Heals, Waring and Liberty led the field with modern designs in chestnut, mahogany, oak, burred oak, sycamore and teak. For the large number who preferred to live in the past, there was an enormous vogue for reproduction Chippendale, Sheraton and Hepplewhite furniture. Queen Anne chairs in walnut were recommended for the then-popular colour schemes of grey, mauve and rose, while Chesterfield settees covered in leather,

If a hall was large enough, coats might be hung away in a cupboard, otherwise they would be hung on a hallstand incorporating mirror, brush set and umbrella stand. A monk's settle had storage under the seat, and a back which could lift to make a table top.

linen or seventeenth- and eighteenth-century style brocades were thought suitable for Queen Anne or white drawing rooms. If you were lucky enough to possess good old furniture, it was thought to go well with reproduction eighteenth-century chairs and sofas. These, in their Edwardian reincarnation, boasted large, comfortable, down-filled cushions that were unheard of in the eighteenth century.

There was a fashion, too, on both sides of the Atlantic for Elizabethan and Jacobean furniture. Messrs Waring and Liberty were renowned for their (far more comfortable) copies of seventeenth-century furniture from Knole, the huge house near Tonbridge in Kent enlarged and adorned by a cousin of Elizabeth I.

As comfort began to take priority, so did practicality. Although silks and brocades remained fashionable, armchairs and sofas with loose covers of flowered chintz became all the rage. Chintz was especially popular when used to accompany reproduction furniture, and ladies were fond of its lightness. An article in *Everywoman's Encyclopaedia* described one very over-the-top room with the mantelpiece covered in chintz, a chintz overmantel and small chintz curtains either side of the fireplace to be pulled across when the hearth was not in use. In addition, it was recommended that the lady of the house match the colour of the chintz to her eyes: mauve or violet-flowered chintz went with blue eyes, but not with green.

As if to complement this *rus in urbe* style, wicker and bamboo furniture also became popular. Wicker chairs with loose covers provided extra seating at small cost; however, some found it creaky, lacking in durability and only suitable for summer houses and verandahs.

Whatever style of furniture one chose for a drawing or living room, no home was complete without a piano, and this had to blend with the remaining furniture. For modern taste, Broadwoods made pianos designed by the architects Ashbee and Lutyens, while for traditionalists there were patterns based on eighteenth-century cabinet-making.

Phonographs or gramophones were gradually being introduced into people's homes, and eventually ousted the piano as a source of home entertainment. For the time being, though, they were regarded as awkward, ugly things that were difficult to fit into an elegant drawing room.

Although in theory the Edwardians wanted to rid their living rooms of Victorian clutter, they remained very crowded. Palm stands vied with jardinieres; Sutherland tables with folding legs and flaps fought for space with two-tier Sheraton tables. Cakes were served from a portable cake stand and would then be eaten from one of a nest of tables dotted around the room, while the teapot was poised on top of a Sheraton-style urn stand.

These illustrations from contemporary furniture catalogues show the variety of styles that were available for reception-room furniture. Reproduction styles were the most common, whether for sideboards, bureaux or bookcases.

RIGHT: *An elaborate fireplace incorporating a mirrored overmantel and two glazed display cabinets shows how inventive the Edwardians could be. The beaten copper hood has echoes of the Arts and Crafts Movement, as does the attractive fibrous plaster ceiling.*

BELOW: *Large bay windows like this one added to the size of reception rooms and often incorporated a window seat.*

Portieres in heavy velvet or brocade had all but disappeared: instead there might be a screen to protect the occupants of a room from draughts. There would be a couple of console or card tables plus the ubiquitous lady's workbasket. The mantelshelf might boast a heavy French gilt bronze mantel clock or a grander one in white marble with electric candelabra to match. A writing desk needed a smaller clock, particularly as the desk might be cluttered with a pen tray, a blotter, a penwiper, a notepad, a letter rack, a paper knife, an inkstand, a box for stamps and a leather case for holding telegram forms. For desks there were tiny clocks in mother-of-pearl, paperweight clocks made from blocks of rose crystal or moss agate, or one of the new electric clocks incorporating an alarm.

Lighting was via tall standard lamps or desk lamps. Thanks to the advent of electricity, there was less danger of fire as both these and the wall or centre lights were electric. The new electric light showed up the walls of the drawing room to best advantage, walls which had plainer paint or wallpaper than during the densely patterned 1880s and 1890s. Now these walls were encrusted with china or paintings.

LEFT: *This modern room cleverly employs one or two touches to recreate a turn-of-the-century feel – the cosy open fire, the old upright piano and the large-faced wall clock.*

ABOVE: *Phonographs were gradually finding their way into Edwardian reception rooms. They often stood on a tall table in a corner where they would not be knocked.*

LEFT: *This fine fireplace with its pilastered surround and double mantelshelf has panels of tiles that show the influence of Art Nouveau.*

The Dining Room

People took the look of their dining rooms very seriously; after all, eating is a serious business. In America in 1918, Richardson Wright remarked that 'To many of us, and particularly to men, dining is the high spot of the working hours. A good dinner works the daily miracle of a man's existence.'

The walls of a dining room were expected to be restful, either with plainly painted plaster or striped wallpaper or, for the Jacobean style, oak panelling. A warm colour scheme with low-toned red paper and olive carpet, or a soft Turkey carpet, was fashionable. A few good oil paintings graced the walls of the dining room and a background of dull red, green or blue was especially popular to set them off. As an alternative to oil paintings, a room with oak panelling and oak beams might be decorated with pewter and blue-and-white china. Oak furniture might be complemented by a floor covering of coarsely woven matting or Persian rugs.

Chippendale or Sheraton-style furniture suited the Queen Anne look, while the panelled room lent itself to Jacobean or Stuart-style furniture. For people tending to the modern or 'artistic' look, William Morris furniture in light oak was thought highly desirable. As always, great care was taken when mixing styles. Richardson Wright demanded co-ordination: 'You cannot put American Colonial with French furniture of Louis XIII, because one is light in scale and domestic in spirit; the other heavy in scale and majestically ponderous in spirit.'

An artistic dining chair might be the solid, old English Windsor chair, or it might be in oak with a rush or hide-covered seat. Period-style chairs would often differ from the originals in having, for reasons of convenience and comfort, lift-out padded seats, often covered in green horsehair.

Tables, like chairs, came in all styles. There were Charles I oak tables with huge bulbous legs, refectory tables, or round mahogany tables with ball and claw feet. As houses now often had smaller rooms and as some people lived in flats, space was often at a premium and gateleg tables or tables with extending leaves became popular. Wolfe and Hollander made the 'Sesame' table, with a concealed extending leaf, which could be bought in Elizabethan, Jacobean or Georgian styles.

To make it easier to achieve the unified, elegant effect people wanted, dining room suites were now being manufactured. Heals produced one in plain or fumed oak called 'The Cottage', a reproduction Jacobean-style suite whose dining table came in two sizes. Sideboards in lighter reproduction styles were easy to move for the room's weekly clean-out. One Queen Anne-style sideboard had a short curtain at the back threaded on a rod held by barley-twist supports, while a Sheraton-style sideboard might have a pair of candelabra at either end. Dressers were popular for oak-panelled rooms, otherwise a simple, inexpensive William Morris-style sideboard would do. The most simply furnished rooms did away altogether with the sideboard and instead had a corner cupboard to store china and glass, and a dinner wagon, butler's tray with stand, or side table for serving.

The lighting at the dining table was all-important: people wanted to be able to see their food without being dazzled. The elegant dining room had electric wall-lights with pink shades,

In the dining room, reproduction styles again held sway; Chippendale chairs became particularly popular. Oak-panelled dining rooms in the vernacular style would be furnished with oak 'Tudorbethan' furniture of the type shown here.

while the table itself was lighted by silver candlesticks topped with thick pink silk shades with a bead fringe. A very modern table had electric table lights connected to a switch in the floor beneath, and these table lights were sometimes fitted so that they nestled among the foliage and flowers of the table decorations. Another popular form of table lighting was a centre light on a pulley that could be lowered to avoid glare in the diners' eyes during the meal.

Beneath the lights, tables were covered in a variety of cloths. A crisp damask cloth was in the best of taste, often with a special American cloth lined with felt underneath to protect the table's surface. Chenille and tapestry cloths were also popular, but according to Mr Elder-Duncan: 'It is impossible to say which is the more hideous, the average dining table or the cloth which usually obscures it. Why householders should consider it necessary to drape their festive boards with the atrocious chenille and tapestry abominations which pass muster for tablecovers is beyond comprehension, but possibly it arises out of the defects of the table itself.' Providing one's table was acceptable, perhaps Mr Elder-Duncan would have approved of the growing vogue for table mats which did away with the need for the endless laundry work associated with tablecloths. Whatever cloth one chose, when entertaining it would be almost totally obscured by gleaming china, glassware, polished silver cutlery and elaborate table decorations.

Libraries and Billiard Rooms

Once the meal was over, the men often played billiards in the oak-panelled billiards room. Smoking rooms had gone out of fashion so the billiards room might include a smoker's cabinet with pipes, tobacco, cigars and cigarettes, as well as a small drinks cabinet. Billiards was such a popular game that almost no house would be without its billiards table, and if the house was too small for a separate billiards room, special tops could be bought to turn a dining table temporarily into a billiards table.

Libraries had good centre lighting as well as a few table lamps and some over-the-shelf lighting. A writing desk was an essential part of the library furniture. If one's work involved a lot of papers, then a pedestal desk, preferably in late eighteenth-century style was preferred; otherwise, a rolltop desk was adequate. The library also often possessed a sofa and several easy chairs, but Mr Elder-Duncan feared that the too easy easy chair induced 'somnolence rather than study'. Bookshelves were either plainly simple or there were grand Chippendale-style bureau bookcases or Adams-style bookcases with open metal-work fronts. Dwarf bookshelves were becoming popular, and the library might also include one or two revolving bookcases.

In general, libraries had a masculine feel, but home decorating books of the day encouraged the addition of photographs, vases of flowers and china cabinets to soften the masculinity. Meanwhile, if there was space, the lady of the house might have a boudoir. This was the female equivalent of the library – her own small sitting room, with two or three chairs, an occasional table, a small bureau or writing table, a settee, a bookcase, and even a small piano or 'pianette'. To possess either a billiards room, library or boudoir was a sure sign of respectability. It also gave Edwardians even more opportunities for furniture and knick-knack buying. The owners of shops and emporia throughout the land were laughing all the way to the bank.

OPPOSITE PAGE: *Three illustrations from a contemporary wallpaper catalogue show the variety of dining-room styles that were popular.*

ABOVE: *The owners of this Edwardian home have chosen to put their dining table in the bay window.*

LEFT: *No self-respecting upper middle-class home would be without its billiards room. It is easy to find reproduction lighting for a billiards table.*

In the hallway of a large Edwardian house, a dinner gong would be an essential item of equipment, along with the hatstand and the umbrella stand. Meanwhile, in the living room, there was an array of furniture ranging from traditional upholstered chairs, settees and chaises longues, to the innovative fumed oak designs for cabinets and pianos by Charles Voysey.

Chapter 3

Stairs, Landings and Bedrooms

'Nowhere in the house is a woman so completely herself as in her bedroom. It is her little domain, and there she is supreme. And it is usually her dream to make it an expression of herself, if so complex a thing as a woman can be expressed – even to herself.'

Richardson Wright, Inside the House of Good Taste, 1918

One immediately obvious difference between an Edwardian house and a Victorian one was that the newly-built homes often no longer had the staircase rising straight up from directly in front of the front door, as they had previously. Now, with wider hallways, the fashion was for a short run of stairs, followed by a small square half-landing from which point the stairs turned to carry on up to the first floor. Nor were stairs any longer being built with the ornate cast-iron newel posts and balusters of the nineteenth century. Turned wooden balusters and a broad, curved handrail were still in vogue, though in the most up-to-date homes, simple square balusters with a squarer newel post and squarer handrail, in the style of Voysey, were fast gaining ground. Sometimes the newel post would be fitted with an electric lamp.

Staircases and Landings

The point at which the hall ended and the stairs began was a difficult area, and one which the Edwardians often tried to soften by the use of fretwork screens or arches hung with drapery. The colour of the walls of the hallway continued up the stairs, and to have a dado or frieze running along the side of the staircase – an effect much loved by the Victorians – was regarded as 'not pleasant' by the early 1900s.

By now the darkness of Victorian halls had given way to light-coloured walls with plain or self-striped papers, and white or cream woodwork. Once the upstairs landing was reached, there were new problems to be faced. Some people furnished an upstairs landing with a table and a couple of chairs, while others thought that landings should simply be left as open and airy spaces, since no-one really wanted to sit there unless they were infirm and needed to rest after climbing the stairs.

The Victorian fashion for landing windows with coloured glass edgings or corners had passed, to be replaced with windows with small leaded panes or, for a touch of colour, roundels or shields of stained glass that could be hung against the plain window. Delft plates on the windowsill were popular and the cosmopolitan influences could be mixed by the addition of a Moorish lamp hanging from a chain. Lightness was everything,

While Charles Voysey advocated simple, square balusters and newel posts, less advanced taste still favoured turned balusters, elaborate newel posts and decorated stair ends. Glass lanterns frequently lit landings and hallways while an upstairs landing might boast a small table or plant stand. In some homes there might be a dado of wood panelling running up the stairs, but in modern homes, wallpaper was more common.

so often there would be no curtain at the landing window, but a bad view could be screened by the thinnest net or muslin.

Bedrooms

The feeling of sunshine, airiness and light was carried on into the bedrooms. If the Edwardians still took themselves rather seriously in their reception rooms, their bedrooms allowed more scope for a light touch. Here walls were almost invariably white or cream, either plain painted plaster, light painted wood panelling, or decorated with floral papers on a light background. There was an abundance of papers featuring hollyhocks, wisteria, roses, laburnum, clover and daffodils, as well as trailing ribbons and bows, trellis designs, baskets and trails of flowers.

The most modern wallpapers in the early years of the century unexpectedly featured black backgrounds, such as William Morris's popular 'Blackthorn'. Dark colours might suit a businesswoman's bedroom that had to serve as a sitting room as well. One of these was described in 1918 by the American Richardson Wright in *Inside the House of Good Taste*. Since, according to Richardson Wright, the businesswoman 'shares with men the abhorrence of frippery and dust-catchers ... it is best to keep to rather dark tones and to make as little of a feature as possible of the bed as a bed'.

Serious, dark-toned rooms such as these were the exception, however, and were regarded as rather 'artistic'. Most people –

OPPOSITE PAGE, ABOVE: *The squarer Edwardian hall meant that the staircase no longer had to rise up straight from directly inside the front door.*

OPPOSITE PAGE, BELOW: *A large window with pastel-toned stained glass lights a staircase.*

THIS PAGE: *Most Georgian and Victorian floor plans were rather cramped, only allowing for rooms to lead off from one side of the staircase. This Edwardian upstairs landing has rooms leading off from both sides, as well as French windows opening onto a balcony.*

*Modern bedroom furniture often
included a washstand with a
tiled splashback to hold a jug
and ewer. The suites of furniture
shown in the two bedrooms here
do not include washstands,
possibly because these homes had
adequate bathroom facilities.
Notice the light touch added to
these bedrooms by the
introduction of a wicker chair.
Chairs like these would have
been unthinkable in a heavily
upholstered Victorian bedroom.*

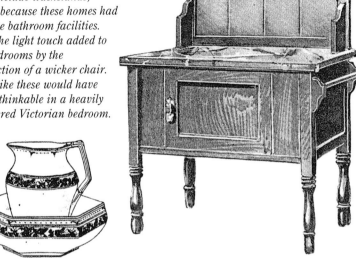

women at least – hankered after a room suffused with 'the spirit of a nosegay plucked from the gardens of the Trianon', a description given by Richardson Wright to a Louis XVI-style bedroom. Such an effect could be obtained by the judicious use of one of the floral wallpapers, together with bedhangings, curtains, chair covers and mantelshelf border made from a floral chintz or cretonne, or from a plain fabric dotted with appliquéd or embroidered flowers.

The furniture which best complemented this look was finished in the very fashionable white enamel or white paint. By the turn of the century, suites of white or natural wood bedroom furniture were common and were available at prices starting from about £4. A typical suite might consist of a bedstead, wardrobe, washstand and dressing table or dressing chest, plus one or two chairs. Larger suites included a couch, shaving table, cheval glass and pedestal tables for the bedside. Old furniture was very sought after and there was a thriving market for good old four-poster beds, tallboy chests and old-fashioned washstands. Some preferred modern furniture, however, which featured washstand tops and backs of hygienic tile or marble.

While suites of furniture were becoming more common, so was fitted furniture. This was popular both as a good space-saving device for smaller modern rooms, and for the purpose of concealing less-than-beautiful items, like the washbasins

RIGHT: *A large mirror framed with neo-Georgian moulding is an unusual feature of this upstairs landing.*

BELOW: *Edwardian 'sweetness and light' is epitomized in the dainty detail of a landing window.*

Lutyens installed behind cupboards at Folly Farm. By World War I there were plenty of fitted wardrobes, some built to nestle in awkward corners, some fitted with drawers long enough to hold a gentleman's trouser stretcher. In addition there were fitted washstands with mirror and medicine cupboard above and boot cupboard below, and fitted cupboards to house suitcases and hatboxes. Fitment furniture such as this was to be found in white enamel, mahogany, fumed oak and Sheraton inlaid wood – in other words, something to suit every taste.

Taking convenience one stage further, and of particular interest to the growing ranks of flat-dwellers, was the availability of multi-purpose furniture – the combined sideboard/bed on castors that looked like a sideboard from the front but which held a made-up bed behind, or the dressing table/washstand/chest of drawers combined, with a towel rail at one end. Another space-saving device was the 'under-robe', a box on castors for clothes storage that slid under the bed, or the 'Bat' and 'Bee' beds that transformed from single to double beds by means of 'ingenious

LEFT: *The simple bedroom fireplace decorated with Art Nouveau motifs is typical of Edwardian rooms that were not on public view.*

BELOW: *A cosy window seat fits neatly beneath the windows of a bedroom turret.*

hinges and unseen folds'. For a gentleman whose wife read *Everywoman's Encyclopaedia*, a washstand/chest of drawers combination with shaving glass attached 'should leave ample space for morning dumb-bell exercise, however small the room may be'.

Other items of bedroom furniture included writing tables and bookcases, while for a man, according to Richardson Wright, there should be a large, comfortable chair by the bedside table which should be 'large enough to hold, beside a serviceable lamp, a pile of magazines and best sellers, for it is thus that most men quiet down for the night'. For gentlemen there were also shaving tables with a nickel-plated shaving set lit by candles or electric light.

A china toilet service consisting of a ewer and basin, soap dish, brush holder and sponge bowl stood on the washstand, while silver-mounted toilet sets – hairbrush and comb, clothes brush, hand mirror, powder-puff jar, pomade jar, brush tray, comb tray, trinket box, curling tongs, glove stretchers and button hook – decorated the dressing table.

In the days before clocks with luminous dials, the problem of seeing the numbers in the dark was one which taxed the Edwardians. J.H. Elder-Duncan tells of an electric bedroom clock in polished wood or leather that reflected the time on the ceiling: 'one only has to press a button and look aloft to see the hours plainly shown on the ceiling above our heads'.

Bedroom lighting was by now largely electric, and included electric lights with moveable shades that could be hung on a hook in the wall at the correct height for reading in bed. Although Mr Elder-Duncan thought that a dressing table and cheval glass should be adequately lighted, he was not so keen on a bedside light, though he conceded that 'many people read in bed, and, though this may not be a desirable habit, there are occasions, as in illness, when it is legitimate'.

The bedroom floor was often of parquet, covered with Persian rugs, rag rugs or occasionally tiger skins. Sometimes there was a large Persian rug covering the floor, with the surrounding floorboards painted white.

Although Edwardian bedrooms were private places, far from the gaze of visitors, the guest bedroom was a different matter and the mistress of the house took a lot of trouble to make it welcoming. Flowery rooms were *de rigueur*, with lilac a very popular colour. Lilian Joy, author of 'The Ideal Spare Room' in *Everywoman's Encyclopaedia,* suggests a tasteful scheme of cream wallpaper with a white stripe decorated with a frieze cut from a lilac-design wallpaper. There were curtains of lilac-patterned cretonne or chintz, with inner casement curtains of mauve linen. The carpet was green and the bedspread natural linen with a spray of lilac-patterned cretonne appliquéd in each corner. A table runner of embroidered and crocheted white and mauve linen decorated the dressing chest, and there was a pin-cushion of embroidered white linen threaded with mauve ribbon for hatpins. The toilet service had a design of lilacs and each drawer of the dressing chest had 'laid at the bottom a muslin bag filled with lavender and decorated with the principal colour used in the room'. There was a writing table, its blotter covered with chintz to match the room, and a comfortable chair in plain linen,

FIG I

While children enjoyed the latest in white enamelled bedroom furniture stencilled with nursery figures, the adults in the house might sleep on a very hygienic metal bedstead or on an elaborate period-style one. A foldaway bed-table or elaborate book stand incorporating a lamp and table were other items to be found in the bedroom.

RIGHT: *The original owners of this Edwardian bedroom would feel perfectly at home with the modern floral wallpaper and fabric, the glass-fronted china cabinet, the Adam-style fireplace and the mixture of furniture styles.*

BELOW: *Built-in bedroom cupboards like these were among the very practical features of English homes that appealed to Hermann Muthesius in* Das Englische Haus.

as well as a large bag for soiled linen and a cardboard hat-box covered with chintz. The china used for early morning tea repeated the prevailing tone of the room. According to Miss Joy, motoring visitors often arrived with very little luggage, so a dressing gown and bath slippers were useful additions. Pretty ornaments, blue and white Oriental china on the mantelshelf and engravings or prints of landscapes by well-known artists completed the tasteful scene. In fact, nothing was left to chance.

In larger homes with children there was a day nursery where the children played and had their meals, and a night nursery where they slept with their nurse. Once again, nothing was left to chance in the decoration of these rooms and uncertain parents were offered plenty of advice in magazines by all manner of experienced midwives, nannies and nurses.

Rule number one for the day nursery was to ensure a healthy location. A room that was either north-facing, facing the street or high up at the top of the house with small windows, extremes of hot and cold and where the small charges would breathe in the used-up air from the lower rooms was unacceptable. Good ventilation was all-important so there was always an open chimney in the room and the sash windows were left open night and day, but a nail in the window frame prevented them from being opened too far for safety. Draughts, though, were another matter and were excluded with special indiarubber draught-excluders, while cracks in the floor were filled with putty or cement.

The ceiling was usually painted white or cream, or was covered with a washable paper. The old-fashioned alternative was to whitewash it every spring. A decorative wallpaper frieze

LEFT: *Another view of the bedroom opposite shows a small oriel window, a design feature taken straight from English vernacular architecture.*

BELOW: *This small bedroom fireplace is decorated with neo-Georgian swags.*

might liven up the walls, or they might be covered in one of the new nursery-rhyme papers. Now there was also specially designed miniature nursery furniture in plain oak or stained wood. The little suites of furniture consisted of small chairs, a table, a comfy sofa, a toy cupboard with low shelves that could be easily reached by the children and a toy table with a raised edge to prevent small toys and marbles falling off.

The nursery floor was warm and washable, often covered with linoleum or cork, and with washable cotton rugs. If a baby was not in one of the new playpens – 'a sort of sheep-fold' according to *Everywoman's Encyclopaedia* – then it might be given a decorated crawling mat to lie on face down. The value of tiny children having colourful shapes and patterns to look at was already being recognized, while the bad effects on children from seeing pictures in the nursery that were crudely coloured or badly drawn were supposed to remain with them for life.

Nurse would have a big cosy chair, a clock, a lockable medicine cupboard, and a dresser-like cupboard to store the children's crockery and cutlery and a few biscuits. Although they ate in the day nursery, their meals were prepared in the kitchen.

A tall fireguard protected them from the fire and any lamps with open flames had a safety apparatus for putting out the flame if the lamp accidentally overturned. Any oil lamps were on the wall well out of the reach of the children, but with electric lights now more common, most of these safety devices were no longer needed.

In the night nursery good ventilation was considered even more important, for poor ventilation was thought to cause sleeplessness in children. The walls and ceiling were painted in a restful colour and the floor was stained and varnished, then polished or covered with parquet or linoleum, with washable rugs on top. A good nurse ensured that there was a rug by the bed of each child so there would be no danger of her inadvertently standing a barefooted child on the cold floor in the middle of the night. The beds themselves – including nurse's – in wood, iron or brass were quite spartan, without any decorative valance or drapery. The base was woven wire with a hair mattress on top, with a waterproof sheet for the youngest, two or three blankets, cotton sheets, a low, soft, hair-stuffed pillow and perhaps an eiderdown quilt. Babies slept in cots with deep sides that could drop down, while older children had half-sized bedsteads. Windows shaded with soft, dark green material that could be washed every week ensured that the children did not wake too early.

As in the day nursery, the night nursery had its set of miniature furniture, but it also needed a full-size clothes-press, a low nursery chair for nurse to sit in while feeding the baby, and a dressing table for her.

The greatest care was always taken with children's health, because many still died young. If children were bathed in the night nursery, there was always a screen to protect them from draughts, and experts recommended that there should not be a bathroom, lavatory or housemaid's sink opposite the nursery door for fear of foul air wafting into the children's room. The image that we have nowadays of children strictly brought up by a stern nanny in spartan surroundings was no doubt a realistic one for many middle-class Edwardian children.

Mirrors, sometimes fitted with the new electric lights, were indispensable in the bedroom. Bookcases were frequently found there, as well as folding screens to protect from draughts. An ottoman would provide extra seating with storage space for bed linen, while boots and shoes might be stowed neatly on a special stand. Baby's crib was usually quite simple, without elaborate flounces to harbour dust and germs.

Chapter 4

Kitchens and Bathrooms

'...there are disappointments in store for the visitor to England who expects really luxurious bath installations like those demanded by well-to-do house-owners on the continent ... The bathroom is always the simple, plain room dictated by need. Everything is of the best, but the room is fundamentally modest and unpretentious.'

Hermann Muthesius, Das Englische Haus, 1904

The illustration from the American Architectural Year Book *of 1911* (BELOW) *shows how simple Edwardian kitchens were. However, the kitchen opposite achieves a period feel while being more suited to today's lifestyle.* ROBINSON & CORNISH

The early years of the twentieth century brought people into the modern world with a bang, and in their homes there were no rooms more modern than the kitchen and bathroom. The mid-nineteenth century had seen several outbreaks of cholera, medicine had made great advances and there was a much better understanding of how disease spread. Everywhere in Edwardian household manuals people were exhorted to ensure thorough cleanliness, with the result that the English middle classes became obsessed with hygiene. England led Europe in its development of the sanitary bathroom, while its kitchen arrangements were unbeatable on the grounds of practicality.

Kitchens

The kitchens Muthesius saw and described were those of large town and country houses. This was the domain of the cook and butler and all their staff: the mistress of the house rarely entered. Here the kitchen was exclusively for the preparation of food, while washing-up was done in a separate scullery leading from which might be one or more larders, a pantry, a washhouse and a butler's pantry where the silver was kept. In addition there was a servants' dining room.

Even beforeWorld War I smaller houses often had a separate kitchen and scullery, while a modest middle-class home had at least one servant who would need somewhere to eat her meals. According to Gladys Owen who wrote 'The Ideal Kitchen' for *Everywoman's Encyclopaedia*, 'if there is not even a tiny room in which the domestics can sit and have their meals, it is advisable to have a larger kitchen, because, otherwise, the valuable maids will soon leave, and the worthless ones, who may condescend to remain, will work specially badly'. By the

Edwardian House Style

end of World War I, however, all that had changed. Newly-built houses were more compact, had electricity and, in the vast majority of cases, were servantless. A small, modern kitchen then became a necessity.

With hygiene at the forefront of their minds, the Edwardians took the decoration of their kitchens very seriously. Walls were painted white or a light, bright colour in a washable paint, and the white ceiling was washed or whitewashed every year. Walls with rounded corners as in hospitals were recommended to avoid dust-traps. Around the sink, on each side of the range and behind the gas stove the walls were covered either with tiles, with galvanized zinc or with enamelled zinc patterned to look like tiles.

Wooden floors were usually covered with linoleum in a pattern of black and white squares, in carpet designs, imitation parquet or 'Tile-oleum' for a red-tile effect. Stone scullery floors were easy to keep clean but cold, noisy and tiring to stand on. A wooden scullery mat was recommended 'since stone floors, damped perhaps with splashings from the sink, are responsible for many chills'.

Extensive dinners and complicated laundry and household cleaning procedures meant that the kitchen and scullery were the real work centres of the Edwardian home. A whole day was often devoted to laundry work, with another day for the ironing. Wringers and mangles took some of the labour out of doing the laundry, and in some homes there were simple forms of washing machines. A multitude of gadgets, including vacuum cleaners, assisted with the household cleaning, while food storage was greatly helped by the invention of refrigerators.

J.B&S.Lª

The sink, whether it hung in the kitchen or the scullery, was made from porcelain or stoneware with one or two grooved, sloping wooden draining boards. A large scullery might have a row of sinks, all with hot and cold water, beneath a row of windows. If, in the larger house, there were no slop sinks on the upper floors, then the scullery might include a separate slop sink, as well as troughs for washing vegetables and fish, and a wash-basin for the staff to wash their hands. The butler's pantry, which by Edwardian times was going out of fashion, would also have a lead-lined sink where glass and china could be washed without danger of damage from other heavier items. Wooden plate racks for draining wet plates hung on the walls above the sinks.

More compact sink arrangements came into use gradually. One triple sink had a bowl for washing, one for rinsing, and a central division for the grease overflow. There were even early types of dishwashers such as the 'Polliwashup'. A metal casing held a removable wire basket for the crockery and cutlery, a kettleful of hot water was added, a handle was turned and, hey presto! a paddle pushed the water against the dishes.

The kitchen range, the largest item in the kitchen, was for cooking food as well as for heating water. Many ranges were designed to provide an open fire, even though this often meant that heat was lost. The English liked to make toast for breakfast on the coals and they liked their meat roasted in front of the open fire. To do this the meat was suspended in a bottle jack which automatically turned it. The result was, according to Muthesius, tasty and not requiring any accompanying sauce, hence sauce-making was rare in English cooking. What English cooking

OPPOSITE PAGE: *Many Edwardian kitchens had built-in dressers but they would not have been quite as decorative as this modern one. The open shelves stored earthenware dishes while beneath, the 'pot board' – often nothing more than another shelf – housed the pots and pans.*
ROBINSON & CORNISH

THIS PAGE, LEFT ABOVE: *A North American kitchen built* c. *1910 incorporates a wooden dresser with glazed cupboards above and drawers and cupboards beneath.*
SPADINA HOUSE, TORONTO, CANADA

LEFT: *The simple painted cupboards of this modern kitchen are very similar to the cupboards of the American kitchen above left. A modern design such as this would suit the kitchen of an Edwardian home.* GREENWICH WOOD WORKS

ABOVE: *A simple wall-cupboard such as this, with plain, glazed doors would also complement an Edwardian-style kitchen.*
CRABTREE KITCHENS

lacked in sophistication though, Muthesius claimed it made up for in the quality of its ingredients.

Many of the cooking ranges at the beginning of the century were very large, with several ovens, warming compartments, a grill and the boiler. Gas cookers had also been introduced and often the kitchen had one of these as well as the range. In summer the gas cooker saved on coal, labour and heat in the kitchen. The early gas cookers were nothing more than a large roasting oven to hold a hanging joint, with gas flames burning all around the inside. After the war, according to R. Randal Phillips writing in *The Servantless House* in 1920, diets became lighter so stoves were more compact. Economy was another factor and cheaper-to-run, cleaner anthracite-burning stoves were available. The Carron company made the 'Colhainer' whose sliding doors combined the cheerfulness of an open sitting-room fire with the features of a small kitchen range. The 'Gascol' was a combination coal range and gas stove, while the 'Wifesjoie' must have brought pleasure to many a wife with its single ring gas cooker that also heated a cylinder of water. Compactness reached a peak of perfection with the 'Multicooker'. This one-ring oil or gas burner had a metal shelf that fitted over the burner. At one end of the shelf were two circular openings to hold saucepans, while the other end was perforated. An open-bottomed oven with shelves fitted over the perforations, so a single burner could heat an oven and two saucepans.

Cooking by electricity was slowly being introduced and in the years immediately after World War I electric stoves were installed in new houses built for workmen. Nevertheless most people carried on heating their water using the coal- or anthracite-burning range in the kitchen, although this was very labour-intensive and dirty. In one plan for a servantless house, the space under the kitchen-sink draining boards was ingeniously fitted with doors enclosing hoppers filled with coal from outside.

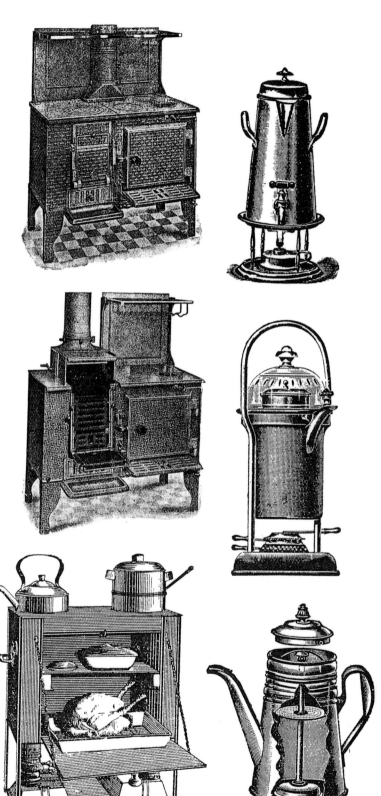

Writing on the subject of 'The Ideal Kitchen' in Everywoman's Encyclopaedia *in 1912, Gladys Owen stated that 'considering that the kitchen department is largely responsible for the health, comfort, good temper, and general well-being of the entire household, it is remarkable that so little time, thought, ingenuity and money are spent upon it'. Judging from the array of kitchen ranges, urns, kettles, percolators and other contrivances that were available, there was no reason, other than cost, for the Edwardian kitchen to be behind the times.*

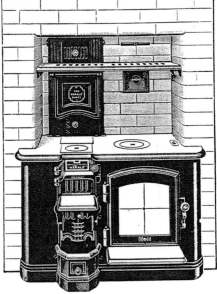

BELOW AND OPPOSITE PAGE, FAR RIGHT: *These grates, each incorporating two ovens, a hob and warming cupboards, would have been the latest thing in Edwardian times. Its modern equivalent is shown below, right.*

Awkward arrangements such as these grew less popular as fewer servants became available. Independent gas-fired boilers for heating water gradually took the place of the kitchen range and eventually gas-heated circulators brought a complete hot-water service to the home, clearing the way for the development of central heating and modern bathrooms.

Back in the kitchen, food was prepared on a large wooden kitchen table. Part of the table might be topped with a piece of marble for pastry-making, or another, small marble-topped table would stand elsewhere. The table was scrubbed daily unless it was covered with galvanized zinc tiles which only needed a wipe with a solution of household soda.

Most cooking utensils were stored on the built-in painted wood dresser, which comprised open shelves for the earthen-ware dishes and a 'pot board' underneath for the pots and pans. A modern, more hygienic arrangement was to store pots and pans on a triangular metal stand in a corner.

Food was kept in tiled larders with wooden or marble shelves. Larger houses had one larder for milk and meat and

OPPOSITE PAGE, RIGHT: *This corner of a modern kitchen has a very decorative built-in dresser.*
ROBINSON & CORNISH

LEFT: *A spacious kitchen with large oven and kitchen table in the centre shows how it is possible to capture the feel of the more spartan Edwardian kitchen using modern designs.*
CRABTREE KITCHENS

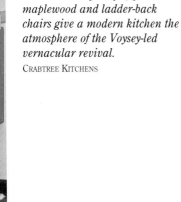

LEFT: *The simplicity of plain maplewood and ladder-back chairs give a modern kitchen the atmosphere of the Voysey-led vernacular revival.*
CRABTREE KITCHENS

another for dry stores. The refrigerator – not much more than a wooden cabinet with shelves holding a lump of ice at the top in a perforated tray – stood here too. As houses became smaller, this proliferation of work surfaces and storage areas could not continue. By 1918 American household manuals showed fitted cupboards with shelves on moveable cleats and ratchets, with built-in cutting boards for bread and meat, and even with a bread-kneading board housed in a deep, zinc-lined drawer. Garbage incinerators were available in America too, especially useful for the many who lived in flats and apartments.

The freestanding kitchen cabinet providing work and storage space in one compact unit was one idea that came to England from America. One incorporated a flour-hopper with sieve, a sugar dispenser, a pull-out enamelled metal worktable, a tin-lined drawer for storing bread and biscuits and an indicator to show what household stores were needed. The English-made 'Quicksey' cabinet had a row of tins or jars for dried goods which automatically opened and closed with the cabinet.

The idea of a kitchen cabinet incorporating storage areas and work surfaces was one that came from America and quickly caught on in Britain, paving the way for modern fitted kitchens. The exteriors of cupboards such as these could be copied by anyone wishing to install an authentic-looking Edwardian kitchen.

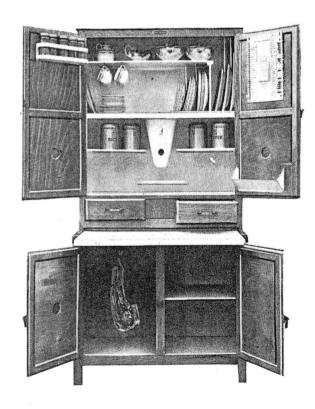

RIGHT: *Modern reproductions of bathroom fittings and tiles can recreate the opulent style that appealed to seriously wealthy Edwardians.* PARIS CERAMICS

BELOW AND OPPOSITE PAGE: *It is unusual to find an original Edwardian bathroom that is still intact like this one in a North American house built c.1911. Here are all the details one would expect – the white ceramic ware, the washbasin on legs, a sitz bath, a practical cupboard above the sink, the gleaming array of taps, the semi-circular shower and, because the owners of this house were extremely wealthy, marble floors and walls.*

Bathrooms

While in 1920 having a 'Quicksey' cabinet in the kitchen may have been considered rather modern, having an up-to-date bathroom with hot and cold running water was far from unusual, at least in the cities. According to Muthesius, 'The presence of a bathroom was taken for granted in England at a time when it was still an exception in the German house.'

For wealthy Edwardians who did not want a 'fundamentally modest and unpretentious' bathroom, the style of Ancient Rome provided some inspiration. At Sir Philip Sassoon's 1925 house at Port Lympne in Kent, together with more traditional features, there were elaborate bathrooms and a Roman-style swimming pool and Moorish patio. Mark Girouard, writing in 1979 in *Life in The English Country House*, described its owner as 'torn between the standards of *Country Life* and Metro-Goldwyn-Mayer'.

For most people, a well-equipped, practical bathroom with separate WC was all that was required, but for older houses or flats without a bathroom, there were ingenious foldaway baths

that tipped up on end and were enclosed in a cupboard. Gas-heated circulatory water systems gradually ousted the old, rather dangerous geysers which had provided hot water for baths and washbasins at the beginning of the century, and modern flush-down toilets with a flushing rim and trap were commonplace.

People living out in the country were not so lucky, for main drainage had not yet arrived. In 1912 Spencer Sills wrote in *Common-Sense Homes: A Practical Book for Everybody,* 'many isolated houses, and, for that matter, many villages and small townships, still use the midden privy for the disposal of the more solid wastes, while the slop-water and kitchen wastes are conveyed to the nearest brook, river or ditch by open channels or roughly made drains of ill-considered design and worse construction'. For such people, the size of one's bathroom and whether it was possible to manage with only one bathroom in a house if that bathroom led off the main bedroom were rather academic questions. For them the 'ridiculously inadequate' 6x4ft bathroom which would 'bring one near to asphyxiation' and would damage the elbows of 'the energetic bather ...

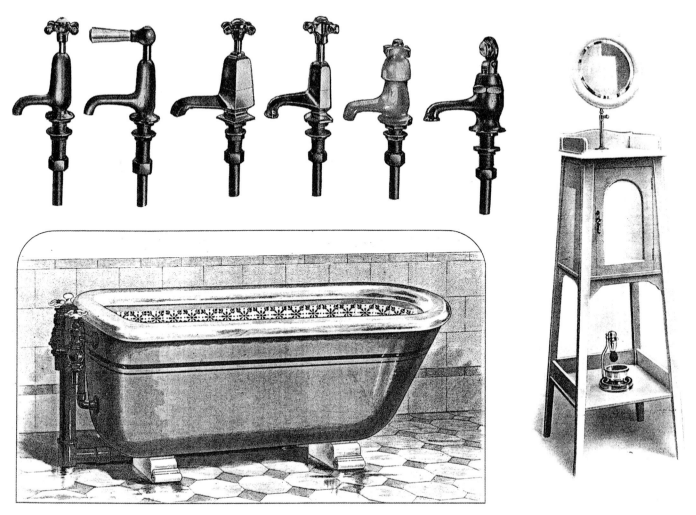

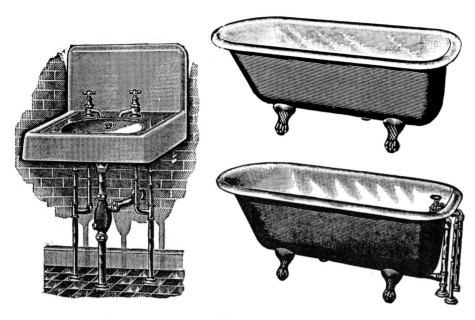

Britain may have been leading Europe in bathroom design, but the Americans were even farther ahead. In his Inside the House of Good Taste *published in New York in 1918, Mr Richardson Wright pointed out that 'what was satisfactory plumbing twenty-five years ago would not be considered so today and that the best we have today will be none too good for tomorrow. This is one department of house-building where it pays to do it correctly in the beginning, and save money and get better satisfaction ever afterwards.'*

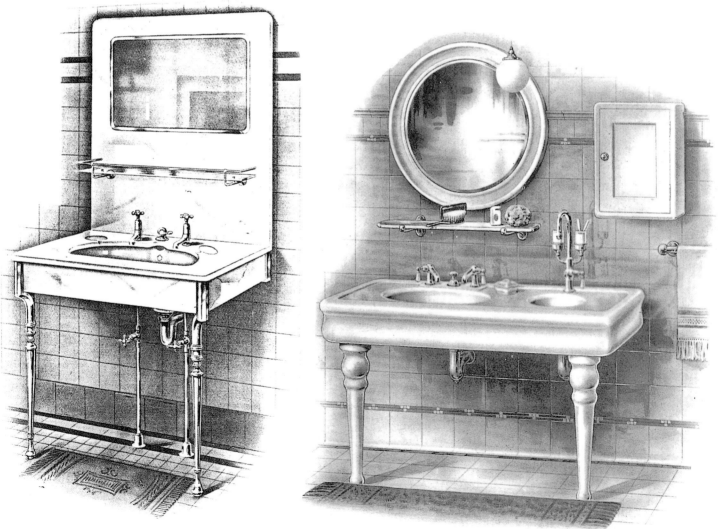

BELOW: *Keeping to a light colour scheme with white fittings recreates the look of an Edwardian bathroom.*
DOULTON BATHROOM PRODUCTS

OPPOSITE PAGE *These copies of white Edwardian ceramic ware with their exposed pipework and freestanding bath are faithful to the originals.* LEFT: COLOURWASH

BELOW: *Copies of Edwardian floor mosaics which, in turn, were taken from Roman designs, would be appropriate for an Edwardian-style bathroom.*
PARIS CERAMICS

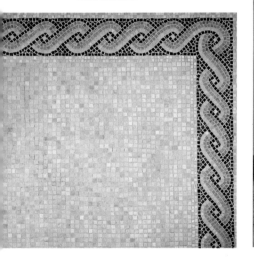

in the towelling stage', as described in *Everywoman's Encyclopaedia,* would have seemed like heaven.

Any modest-sized bathroom had considerable condensation problems so its walls were either painted with a washable paint or tiled, if not up to dado height, then at least round the bath and washbasin. For those who could not afford dado-height tiling or for people in rented accommodation who did not want to invest money on something they could not take with them, a cheaper alternative was the popular tile-effect enamelled zinc. A linoleum or cork-carpeted floor completed the rather clinical look, a far cry from the large late Victorian bathrooms with their wallpapered walls, decorated porcelain basins and rich wood-panelled bath surrounds and washbasin cabinets. Condensation in the smaller Edwardian bathrooms meant that wood had to be banished, while considerations of hygiene demanded that baths and wash basins be freestanding, with their pipework exposed for easy cleaning.

Plain white ceramic ware took the place of patterned ware by

the early 1900s, while baths, either equal-ended or, to economize on water, taper-ended, were made from porcelain or enamelled cast iron. Householders were advised to install a separate sink in the bathroom for the maids to fill their water cans, to avoid their damaging the surface of the bath by resting the cans in it. If the floor beneath the bath was not washable, then it would stand on a lead base to catch any splashes.

A shower could either be attached to the bath or could be separate. If separate it stood on a flat porcelain or marble basin surrounded by a waterproof curtain; if attached, the curtain might be replaced by a semi-circular zinc surround. Taking a shower was a sybaritic experience. The water poured down from above through a (by modern standards) huge rose, flowed around the body through semi-circles of finely-pierced pipe, and could even jet up from below.

The old, unhygienic tip-up washbasins in wooden cabinets were superseded by immense porcelain basins on metal brackets or legs, either set against the wall or, for greater hygiene, wholly

detached from it. Legs and brackets were of brass or nickel-plated brass, and taps were nickel-plated or silver-plated bronze. Without servants to polish them, brass taps fell out of favour. In *The Servantless House* readers are advised to look for china enamelled taps or to paint their brass taps with japan black or 'Adamantine'.

Hot-water circulation systems meant that bathrooms could now have heated towel rails, or alternatively a central-heating radiator might have a towel rail fitted round it. Otherwise towels hung on rods fixed to the wall and a hand towel might hang from a towel roller behind the door. Wood or nickel-plated sponge and soap dishes hung over the side of the bath, while inside the bath an indiarubber mat prevented slipping. A bath step fixed to the outside of the bath helped people in and out, and a cork or towelling bath mat would be waiting for them afterwards. A bell over the bath could be rung if a servant was needed.

Above the washbasin there was a nickel-framed mirror together with a glass shelf on nickel brackets holding a carafe, tumblers and toothbrush holder. The only other furniture was probably a bathroom chair with a cane seat. One bathroom chair in white-painted wood with a cork seat and back was apparently something of a novelty at the Building Exhibition at Olympia in 1911.

And so it was in Edwardian times, with the most up-to-date bathroom fitments – flushdown toilets, foldaway baths, hygienic showers – and every detail in the bathroom designed to provide comfort and convenience at every turn, that England yet again led the rest of Europe.

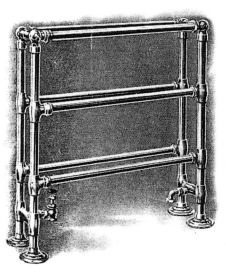

New suburban houses with mains drainage and flush toilets were easier to run than the old Victorian and Georgian homes. This made them attractive to the rising middle classes who might only be able to afford one servant. Shower systems could be very elaborate while the height of modernity was to have a heated towel rail connected to the hot-water system.

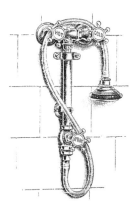

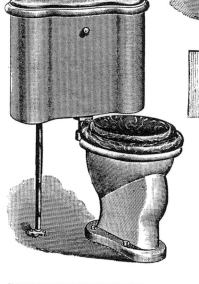

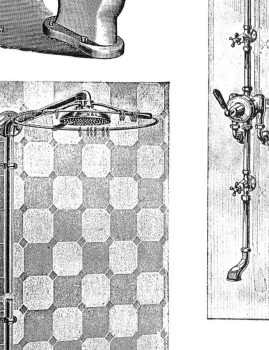

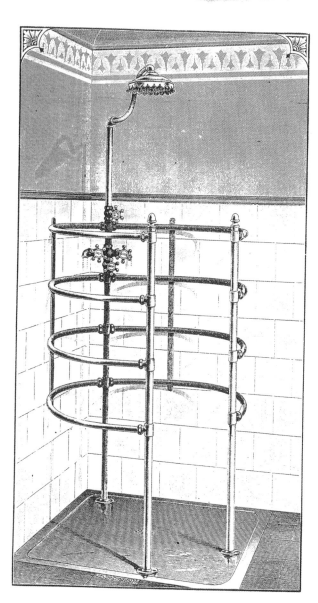

Chapter 5

Interior Details

'Is it not a fact that many of our newer and "cottagey" dwellings are more or less shams, and that what on one hand appears to be the simplest of houses ... often contains a drawing room, dining room, billiard room, study and servants' hall? And that, on the other hand, the interior decoration of many small cottages, or weekend houses, is often carried out on a scale suitable for a ducal mansion?'

J.H. Elder-Duncan, The House Beautiful and Useful, 1907

OPPOSITE PAGE: *This room has many Edwardian interior details that can be copied today. There is a fireplace with Art Nouveau and plain glazed tiles, a wooden floor covered by an oriental rug, and a door with horizontal panels and Art Nouveau finger-plates.*

BELOW: *Walls and furniture were frequently given the floral treatment. Here a lilac wisteria wallpaper frieze complements the tones of the chintz-covered sofa. A pagoda-style lampshade adds a touch of chinoiserie.*

During the Edwardian age the art of interior decoration, previously the preserve of the rich, came within the reach of the middle classes. Household manuals gave advice on everything from how to embroider a candle shade, to how to fold a table napkin. Simplicity appeared to be the keynote, with woodwork now in fresh, white 'flatted' paint instead of grained and varnished as previously, and with furniture thinned out so that it was easier to pick one's way through a room. But beneath the simplicity lay a bewildering range of choices, all of which had to be made according to the rules. It was no good mixing a Sheraton-style china cabinet with a piano in an ebonized case, or hanging oil paintings with watercolours and prints. If you had not inherited good taste along with a houseful of old English furniture, you needed some guidance.

Walls and Ceilings

Walls underwent significant changes to their decoration during this period. In the 1870s, Charles Eastlake in *Hints on Household Taste* had recommended dividing the wall horizontally into three areas: first came a dado, above that a filling and above the filling a frieze or cornice. By about 1910, to have both dado and frieze was considered overdone. Instead there might be a patterned paper up to dado height with the wall above either distempered or plainly papered, or a dado of simple wood panelling painted white, with paper above, to ceiling height.

Wood panelled dadoes had been popular at the end of the nineteenth century, particularly in busy hallways to protect the walls against scuffing, and they continued in popularity in the early years of the twentieth century, as *Roberts' Illustrated Millwork Catalog* published in Chicago in 1903 shows. Here 'paneled wainscoting' in oak or with white pine stiles and rails and yellow pine panels is available.

Whole rooms panelled in wood were admired, but a cheaper alternative was 'Tudoresk' panelling consisting of panels of wood nailed to the wall with a framing overlaid to give the appearance of genuine wood panelling. Meanwhile, for those with more slender means another alternative, especially popular for drawing rooms, was to divide the walls vertically, using 'skeleton panelling' filled with panels of wallpaper or brocade.

Wallpaper was a godsend as a means of covering walls artistically and relatively cheaply, and it was even possible to use speciaally designed papers to create the effect of a frieze, filling and dado. One of these had a frieze of pink roses climbing up a light trellis with, just above the skirting, a similar band which was narrower and with more foliage (the dado). Finally, connecting the two came the filling – a paper consisting of vertical narrow bands of rose and trellis.

Plainer papers with stripes or small all-over patterns were available too, as well as relief papers, designed to be coloured and gilded. These were made from wood-pulp, *papier-mâché* or stiffened canvas and they had evocative names like Lincrusta,

Wallpapers reached new heights of ingenuity in Edwardian times. As seen below, walls were often divided into wallpapered panels, topped with deep, elaborate friezes that were painted, stencilled, or papered. A more traditional effect was achieved using a wallpaper with matching frieze (OPPOSITE PAGE, ABOVE), *while, for the first time, papers specially designed for children's rooms were available* (OPPOSITE PAGE, BELOW). *Fibrous plaster mouldings, cornices and ceiling roses were popular, as they had been in the previous century, but designs were simpler.*

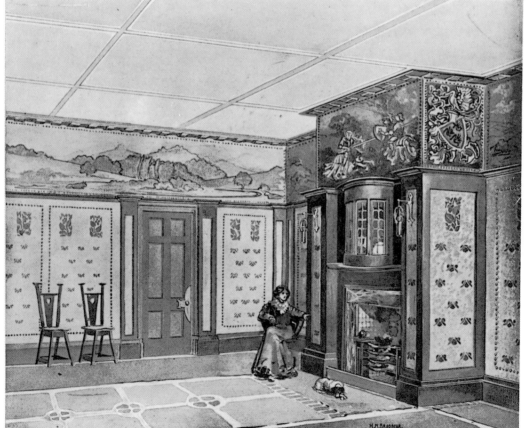

Salamander, Cordelova and Tynecastle. From America came woven wall-coverings as well as imitation tapestry papers, both of which might well have appealed to those with a taste for Jacobean furnishing.

In the late nineteenth century William Morris and Walter Crane brought new vigour to wallpaper design, but by 1907 Mr Elder-Duncan found their patterns 'restless'. He went on to say that 'Morris's "Bruges" paper is a marvel of designing, so is the "Peacock" paper of Walter Crane, but I am very sure I should not care to live with either of them.' Elder-Duncan's particularly demanding taste also excluded the then-popular wood-, marble- and tile-effect wallpapers. No doubt people continued to buy them despite these warnings.

There were almost as many different ways of decorating ceilings as there were of decorating walls. Muthesius summarized what was on offer: timbered ceilings, grid-patterned ceilings, fibrous plaster, relief ceiling papers and stucco-work. In addition, there were ceilings covered with glass mosaic or

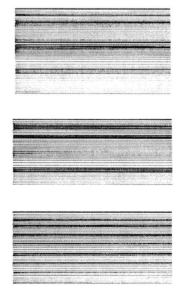

THIS PAGE: *The fashion for 'cottagey' wood panelling was inspired by the Arts and Crafts Movement. Popular for dining rooms, green-toned wood and furniture was thought especially 'arty'.*

THIS PAGE: *The 'Guinevere' wall-paper* (FAR LEFT) *consisted of a background paper and a dado decorated with a landscape, to which were added as many trees – available by the length– as required. The Midsummer Night's Dream* (LEFT) *was a frieze comprising a choice of lengths with landscape and lengths with figures. The Jacobean look* (BELOW) *could be achieved using a combination of panelled wooden dado, panels of wallpaper and a fake plaster frieze.*

stamped steel. This latter could be made to look like old plaster. Ease of application was one of its merits, and the ability to cover damaged plaster effectively was another. Mr Elder-Duncan reluctantly came to the conclusion that it might have its uses in kitchens, bathrooms and sculleries.

The timbered ceiling – part of the vernacular revival – was very popular although could make a room low and dark. Oak beams were the most popular, sometimes darkened with stain, sometimes left natural, sometimes – especially in drawing rooms – painted white.

The grid-patterned ceiling was inspsired by the Elizabethan period. Here the smooth plaster surface was subdivided by a pattern of flat, slightly protruding wooden battens and the whole ceiling was painted white.

The 'fibrous plaster' mentioned by Muthesius was in fact a type of *papier-mâché* that had been pressed into a mould. The panels gave the look of all-over plasterwork without the expense, and was a very popular ceiling finish to accompany reproduction eighteenth-century furniture. Relief ceiling papers gave a similar effect at less cost, while stucco could range from expensive freehand work to the setting of ready-cast sections into the wet plaster of a ceiling. The designs were often attractive, primitive-looking flowers, fruit and foliage cast from seventeenth- and eighteenth-century vernacular originals. Sometimes cornices were extended into deep plasterwork friezes that were painted or stencilled, but the same effect could be achieved more cheaply with a printed or relief wallpaper.

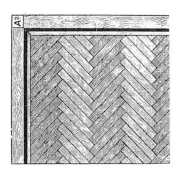

Fitted carpets fell from popularity on both sides of the Atlantic, with the American Mr Richardson Wright declaring that 'the fitted carpet is seldom seen outside a dressmaker's show-room'. Floors were now covered with large squares, or with a number of rugs and runners, the most popular designs being oriental ones. Design-conscious householders took care that carpets with a central motif were reserved for the drawing room where the pattern could be appreciated, rather than the dining room where it would be concealed by a table. Parquet flooring was now very popular as a foil to the new carpet squares, and was available in a wide range of herringbone and basket-weave patterns.

Flooring

The manufacture of and trade in English carpets had been one of the triumphs of the nineteenth century when fully-fitted carpets in strident colours and naturalistic flower, animal and even landscape designs were fashionable. The subdued colourings and stylized plant patterns of Morris, Voysey and Crane were in sharp contrast to these earlier designs, but Muthesius found them distinctly unmodern compared with carpet design on the continent.

As concern for hygiene grew, so the fashion for fitted carpets passed and people favoured carpet squares with a strip of exposed flooring around the edges, or wooden floors covered with rugs. In the United States, the strip around the carpet was sometimes covered with floorcloth printed in a tile pattern. In England this strip would be painted, or covered with felt, lino, matting or parquet.

In Victorian times carpets had been made of strips sewn together and edged with a border to make a carpet of any size. Now larger one-piece carpets were being made. Fashions in carpet design were also changing, as the London store of Liberty found, and the modern designs by Morris, Crane and Voysey were gradually ousted in favour of neo-Georgian patterns in subdued tones of greys, greens and blues designed to complement reproduction furniture.

Turkish, Persian and Indian carpets specially made for the European market were also very popular, offering hand-knotted carpets at prices that English manufacturers could not beat. The English companies retaliated by offering machine-made copies of Oriental designs which are still in production today.

For covering large areas there were other alternatives. Japanese jute and Indian matting were a foil to Persian or Indian rugs. They were cheap, but faded easily. Felt floor coverings came plain or patterned. The patterned variety was not very smart, but the plain one showed every mark and water-stain. For staircases, the most popular carpets were either Turkish or plain, deep-coloured carpets with a velvety pile.

Linoleum continued as an alternative to carpeting, but not for middle-class reception rooms. A thicker form – cork carpet – with a higher cork content, was softer with a matt finish, while the thinner oil- or floorcloth was used in workmen's cottages and cheaper suburban homes.

Whatever the floor covering, the hearth-rug was indispensable and was often the showpiece of the floor. At a time when conservation issues were unheard of, the hearth-rug might be an animal skin.

Wooden floors covered with rugs had long been appreciated on the continent and were now becoming acceptable in England. Floorboards were stained and waxed, or replaced with new tongue-and-groove boards. Parquet was also popular and had the advantage of being available in panels that could be removed by tenants when they moved house.

Woodblock on concrete was coming into use, particularly for kitchens and passages. It was popular with the hygiene-conscious English because there were no spaces between the wood and the ground beneath to harbour dirt and germs. One new flooring was 'Stonwood', made from sawdust or wood pulp, that could be coloured and patterned, sometimes to mimic marble or mosaic. It was laid without joins, was impervious to moisture and was quiet to walk on.

Stone floors were often still found in kitchens, larders and passages, but encaustic tiles which had been so popular in the late nineteenth century gradually fell from favour as they no longer suited the less florid Edwardian home.

Oriental rugs on a plain polished floor were popular in many rooms, but especially in hallways and panelled dining rooms. In 1911, Joseph Wild & Co. of Fifth Avenue, New York, advertised the antique Daghestan rug on the right, but most people had to content themselves with cheaper, modern versions, such as those made in Turkey especially for the European market. In Voysey's hands (OPPOSITE PAGE, LEFT) *the red Turkey rug on a polished floor achieves a lightness that epitomizes the break with Victorian traditions.*

Internal Doors and Door Furniture

Good hardwood doors were too expensive for most middle-class people, while the deal door of the nineteenth century, stained and polished to resemble mahogany, was going out of fashion. Help was on hand in the form of the 'Gilmour' door from Canada, which consisted of a softwood core cased in hardwood, the forerunner of so many modern doors nowadays. The 'Gilmour' had 'an important advantage from the decorator's point of view', for each side could have a different hardwood finish.

Many door handles were in the same styles as during the previous century, but a new fashion arose for long, vertical handles incorporating a finger plate. The English preference for door knobs, as noted by Hermann Muthesius in Das Englische Haus, *may be seen from this collection of contemporary designs, none of which could be opened by a maid carrying a tray using her elbow. A large number of designs similar to these are still manufactured, making it possible to re-create the door furniture of Edwardian times in a period home.*

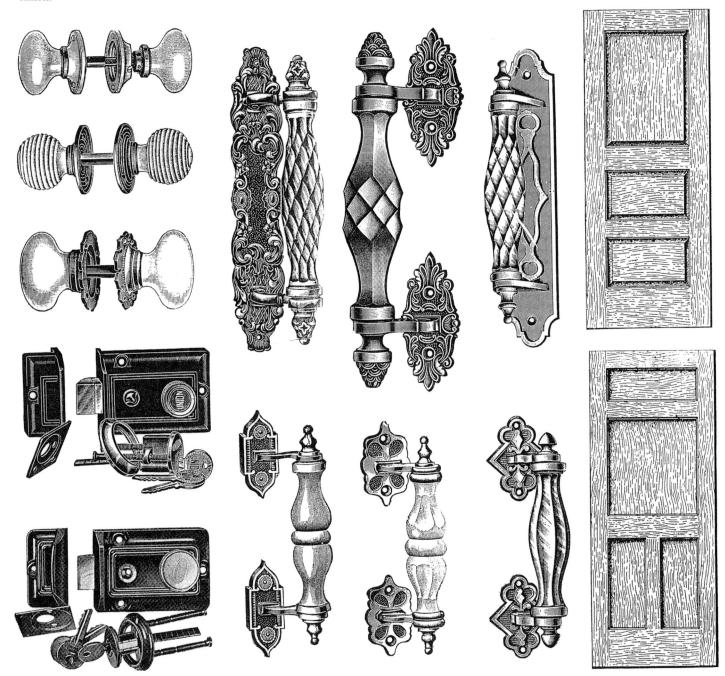

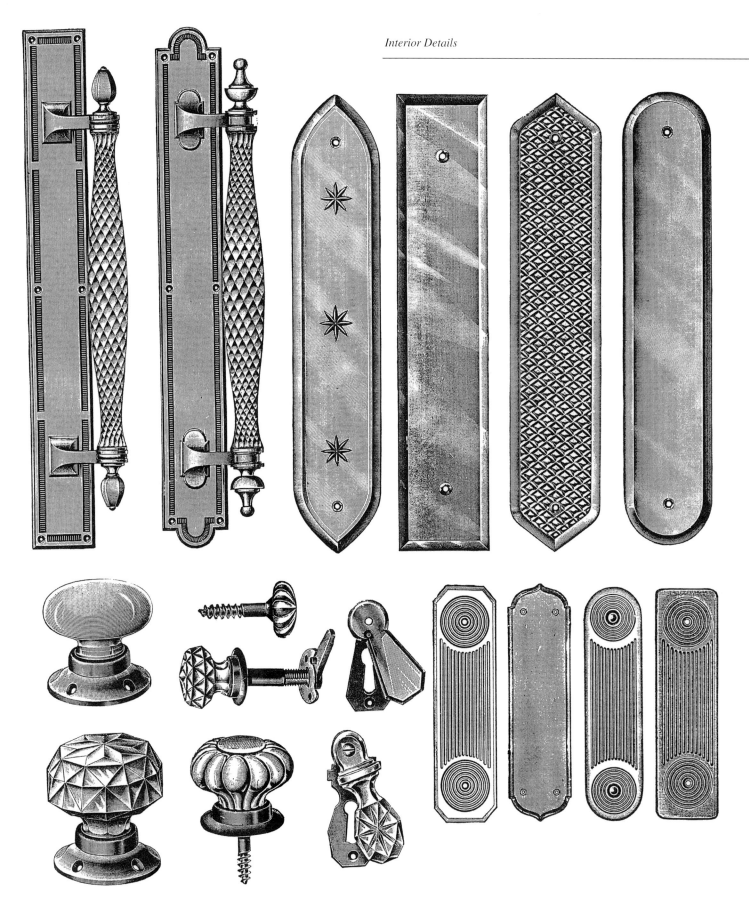

Doors were no longer the simple four-panelled affairs of the nineteenth century. They now sometimes consisted of two vertical lower panels with two horizontal panels above, or they might have stained and leaded glass in the upper panels. Typically, in the house he designed at Tooting, London in 1901, Voysey produced a very idiosyncratic version of a panelled door with glazing (OPPOSITE ABOVE).

For some people the passion for painting one's doors with flowers and other motifs continued, a hangover from the end of the nineteenth century. Mr Elder-Duncan deplored the look: 'The aesthetic craze imbued numbers of well-meaning people with a desire to paint sunflowers on their door panels, and this obsession continues in a mild form to the present day'.

Door furniture came in many materials – china, glass, wood and all sorts of metals. For the rich there was even silver, or enamelled metal set with semi-precious stones. Muthesius admired the English fingerplates, but could not understand the fashion for door knobs rather than handles, remarking that in Germany a maid entering a room with a fully laden tray could at least open the door using her elbow, while in England the maid would have to put the tray down.

BELOW: *Elongated Art Nouveau plant forms decorate these beaten copper fingerplates and door knob.*

LEFT: *Unusually long hinges in wrought iron were a common feature of doors in homes designed by Voysey, often ending in the heart-shaped motif that he liked so much.*

Windows, Blinds and Curtains

Casement windows were better suited to vernacular styles, but with the Georgian revival, the sash crept back into fashion despite its inconveniences. One of these had been the difficulty of cleaning, so various devices came into use to enable the window to be opened inwards, either by hinging the whole window. or by giving it a hinged action as well as a sliding one.

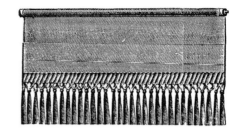

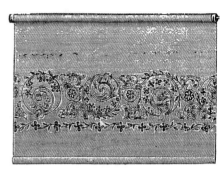

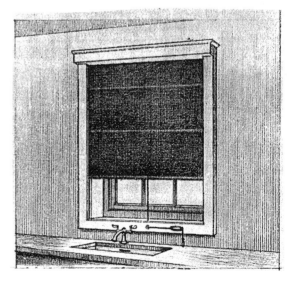

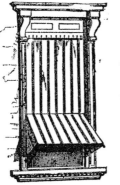

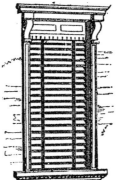

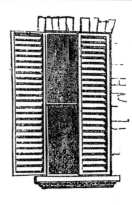

Although full-length lace curtains had fallen from favour, there were still plenty of designs available, made from Nottingham, Swiss, French and Guipure lace. Modern homes had frilled or plain Madras muslin at the windows, like the casement curtains below, while frilly, draped pelmets and valances had given way to plain shaped, or pleated ones. Roller blinds were popular as they were not dust traps, and these came in many plain and patterned fabrics. Blinds and external shutters were sometimes fitted to protect from excessive sun and dust.

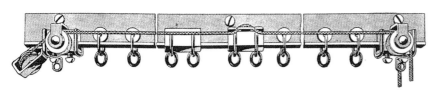

Casement windows were objected to because of the draughts they caused when open so, according to Muthesius, their use was restricted to French windows opening onto a terrace or balcony. The fixed window instead became a favourite in new houses. Here the window was entirely fixed in a stone or wooden frame and only certain lights hinged open.

Stained glass continued to be used for front doors, but as the fashion grew for light interiors, so lighter styles and colours crept into use, often for landing windows and for the upper lights in reception and bedroom windows as well. The influence here was undoubtedly the Glasgow School of Art and the result was glass in more delicate tones of pink, green and amber, with windows sometimes leaded and with small touches of colour here and there. By contrast, there was also a fashion for brightly coloured heraldic designs in stained glass, lending the appearance of aristocratic roots and good breeding to people who had only recently made it to the middle classes.

Inside, the quest for light and sunshine continued. Elaborate pelmets or valances, heavy gilt poles and velvet or brocade curtains with a multitude of drapes, flounces and festoons had, according to Mr Elder-Duncan, 'fortunately gone out of fashion, and it is to be hoped they will never return'. Instead, sash windows had simple brass curtain poles with floor-length chintz

OPPOSITE PAGE, ABOVE: *A window seat fills the space beneath a run of leaded, fixed and casement windows in this house in Tooting, London designed by Voysey.*

OPPOSITE PAGE, BELOW: *At the turn of the century the Swedish artist Carl Larsson depicted his light, airy house in a series of watercolours. These curtains, bedspread and bed hangings would not have been out of place there and are easily copied.*

LEFT: *The original owners of this living room in Hampstead Garden Suburb were likely to have had plain sill-length curtains, but the overall look is quite authentic.*

ABOVE: *These short cotton curtains with simple frilled valance are very much at home in an Edwardian-style kitchen.*

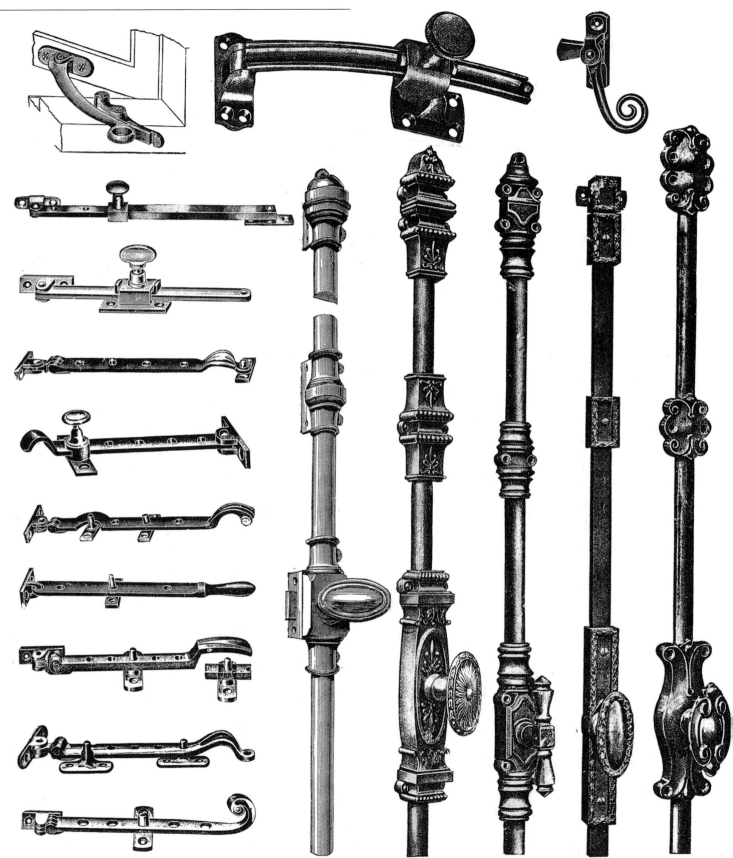

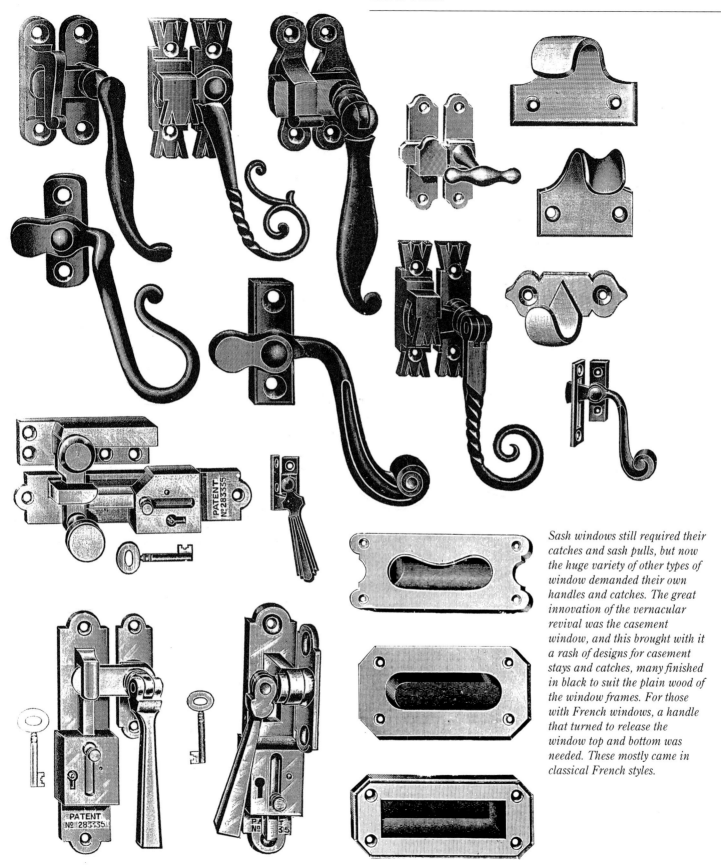

Sash windows still required their catches and sash pulls, but now the huge variety of other types of window demanded their own handles and catches. The great innovation of the vernacular revival was the casement window, and this brought with it a rash of designs for casement stays and catches, many finished in black to suit the plain wood of the window frames. For those with French windows, a handle that turned to release the window top and bottom was needed. These mostly came in classical French styles.

curtains with a white or off-white background, or curtains of damask, silk, wool or tapestry.

Full-length lace curtains underneath the main curtains were now only found in old-fashioned homes, though there might sometimes be a 'short blind' of muslin or lace hung next to the lower pane of a sash window. Houses with casement or fixed-frame windows needed a different treatment and here window-sill-length curtains in chintz, damask or tapestry were the answer.

Various types of blind were still fashionable for the tall sash window. Roller-blinds of stout, semi-glazed material as well as Venetian blinds were common. Other alterantives were a striped linen blind that folded up into a box at the top of the window frame, or a disposable 'Japan' paper blind that was supposed to be destroyed when it got dirty and replaced with a new one.

OPPOSITE PAGE: *Edwardian stained glass was less oppressive than during the previous century, with more pale-toned glass, and sometimes large expanses of plain glass to offset the coloured areas.*

THIS PAGE: *Casement windows required a new approach to window catches. Voysey's wrought-iron casement stay and window catch are uncompromisingly bold.*

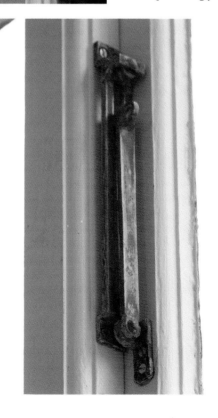

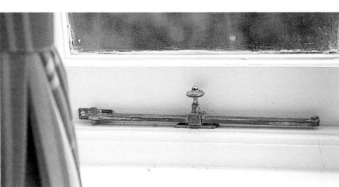

Fireplaces

Muthesius remarked that the English were devoted to their open coal fires and that a room without one was unthinkable. Stoves were not as popular in England as they were in America and on the continent, nor were gas fires, partly because gas was thought to be unhealthy and partly because it was four times as expensive as coal. Sometimes a gas fire was installed in a bedroom to provide rapid heat, otherwise gas was only used to make the clay and asbestos of imitation coal or log fires glow. Electric fires had been introduced, but these were even less popular than gas, despite a Belling model of 1912 which incorporated a kettle and toast rack.

Open fires burned inefficiently so fireplace designers were always trying to improve their designs. By the turn of the century grates were often made of heat-retaining fireclay instead of metal, and had a back that sloped forwards and sides that splayed outwards, all to throw more heat into the room. The fireplace surround was frequently decorated with heat-retaining tiles, the flamboyant patterns of the late nineteenth century giving way to monochrome or Delft-style tiles.

Cast-iron chimneypieces painted white were very fashionable, but were mostly kept for bedrooms. In drawing rooms chimneypieces in stone and wood were used, often in revivals of Georgian styles to complement the neo-Georgian furniture. Wooden mantelshelves became very elaborate dust-traps, sometimes incorporating a central mirror and little shelves either side, or with a glass-fronted cabinet. There were even bookshelf chimneypieces with bookshelves running down the jambs on either side of the fireplace.

The whole fireplace might be turned into a 'cosy corner' with bench seating running along the side wall into the recess formed by the protruding chimneybreast. An arch linking the recess to the chimneybreast together with the walls of the recess faced in wood panelling or brick completed the cosy image. An even cosier effect was achieved with an inglenook fireplace which gave the feeling of a room within a room. Here the fireplace was flanked by walls projecting into the room, and there might also be a canopy above. Bench seating covered with embroidered cushions ran along the projecting walls. Inglenooks were so popular that ready-made inglenook fitments could be bought.

There was a huge market for fireplace accessories of every kind. Fenders came in pierced metal, sometimes tall and upholstered to provide extra fireside seating, sometimes enclosing the entire hearth for nursery use. As well as a coal scuttle there might be a brass stand for a kettle as well as brushes, pokers, shovels and tongs of every description, many of which, according to Muthesius, were left unused to save on cleaning.

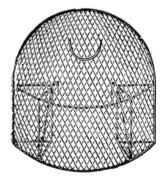

The focal point of many Edwardian rooms was the large open fire which took on even greater proportions when turned into a cosy, inglenook corner like the one above. Gas heating was slow to catch on, but there was an early form of the gas coal-effect fire which consisted of a pierced gas pipe in the grate covered by a piece of iron netting and lumps of coke. The gas was lit for ten or fifteen minutes and ignited the coke. When the fire needed reviving, the gas was turned on again. Muthesius was scornful of the number of fireplace accessories in the English home: 'The three implements, the tongs on one side, the poker and shovel on the other, either lean against the fender in front of the fire or against special supports, called firedogs...So that they shall not slide out of place and become untidy...a piece of metal resembling a paperweight is laid in the middle between them. Thus...the small space inside the fender is almost entirely taken up with useless implements.'

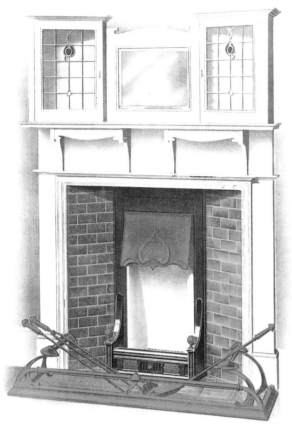

Deep overmantels, and surrounds covered in plain red or green glazed tiles or briquettes distinguished Edwardian fireplaces from their predecessors. Voysey, of course, broke all the rules. A deceptively simple fireplace at an angle in the corner of a bedroom (OPPOSITE PAGE, LEFT) has the natural grandeur of a stone surround such as might have been seen in English manor houses. This is offset by the slender black wrought-iron supports to the mantel shelf. The hall of the same house boasts a simple wood-panelled inglenook fireplace, with seating on either side. This was an idea that was borrowed - and diminished - by anonymous architects everywhere for the next forty years.

Lighting

In the 1890s gas lighting was criticized for making diamonds look dull, while electric light was thought harsh and uncompromising. The old yellow flickering gas flame had been replaced by the steady white light of the incandescent gas burner, but in country areas where there was no gas or electricity, acetylene gas lighting was used, which gave out an unpleasant, intense white light.

By Edwardian times electric light was here to stay. In the rush to design fittings for electric lights, designers neglected gas light fittings although there was still a huge demand for them. As a result, according to Mr Elder-Duncan, 'An inspection of a gasfitter's catalogue is a revelation in the horrible.' The designs for electric light were hardly better. Until the 1920s most light fittings were modelled on the old gas ones, or on earlier styles such as Georgian candelabra or seventeenth-century lanterns, designs which are still in production today. The only other styles were the stylized flower shapes inspired by Art Nouveau or the mosaic glass shades popular in America.

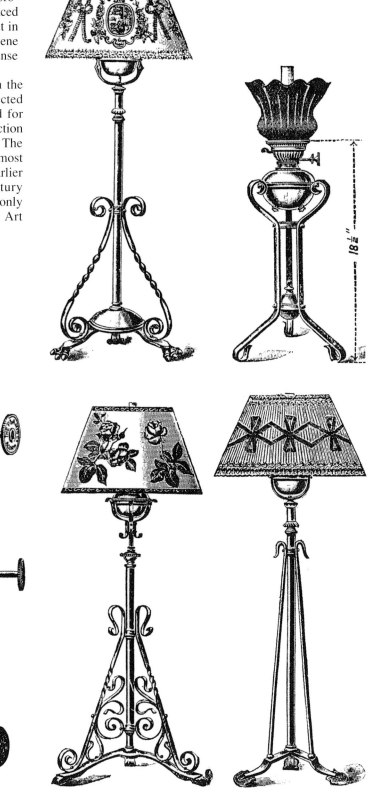

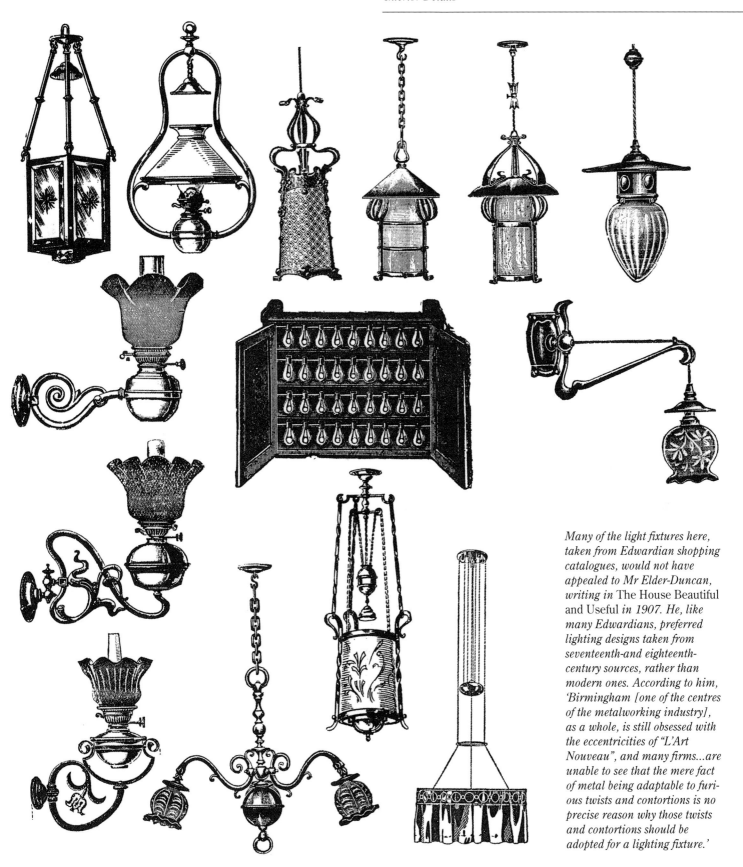

Many of the light fixtures here, taken from Edwardian shopping catalogues, would not have appealed to Mr Elder-Duncan, writing in The House Beautiful and Useful *in 1907. He, like many Edwardians, preferred lighting designs taken from seventeenth-and eighteenth-century sources, rather than modern ones. According to him, 'Birmingham [one of the centres of the metalworking industry], as a whole, is still obsessed with the eccentricities of "L'Art Nouveau", and many firms...are unable to see that the mere fact of metal being adaptable to furious twists and contortions is no precise reason why those twists and contortions should be adopted for a lighting fixture.'*

RIGHT: *Rise-and-fall pendant oil and later electric lights were very common for use over a dining table.*

BELOW, LEFT: *Oil-burning table lamps were cumbersome, with reservoirs, wicks, mantles, chimneys and shades. Electricity made possible the use of safer, more compact fitments.*

BELOW, RIGHT: *Gas-powered ceiling lights always needed a central tube to convey the gas to the fitting. With electricity there was greater scope for dainty hanging chains through which the wire could be threaded, while some fitments were simply suspended from the silk-covered wire.*

LEFT: *The advent of electric lighting meant that there was a demand for accessories like ceiling roses to conceal the wiring, and light switches.* (STIFFKEY LAMP SHOP) *Edwardian lighting could encompass bronze statuettes with glass shades* (BELOW, LEFT) *and telescopic floor lamps with shades in silk* (BELOW, RIGHT). *Floor lamps sometimes had as many as three lights attached.*

Reproductions of Edwardian-style lighting can easily be obtained. They range from simple glass coolie shades (ABOVE), *to the highly decorative stained-glass shades inspired by the designs of the Louis Comfort Tiffany* (ABOVE CENTRE). CHRISTOPHER WRAY'S LIGHTING EMPORIUM

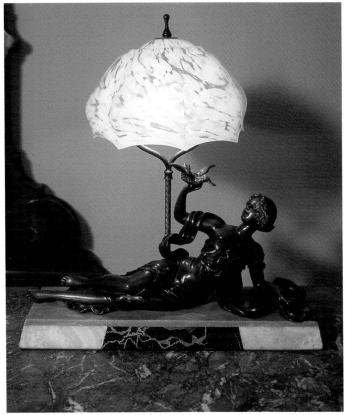

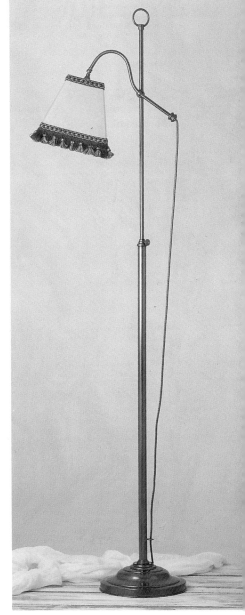

The Edwardians, in their excitement over the new electric lighting, had a tendency to put it everywhere, tucking rows of bulbs behind a reception-room cornice, illuminating picture rails and architraves, wiring Sheffield plate candlesticks to decorate a dining room and even swathing with silk shades the coloured glass bulbs made for exhibitions and outdoor use.

Lampshades were everywhere: deep yellow and rose pink silk for a soft glow, red for dark rooms with panelled walls, beaded shades for a feminine look. There were shades on desk lamps, on standard lamps, on wall lamps and on table lamps, and if the bought shades were not to one's liking, household manuals such as *Everywoman's Encyclopaedia* showed how to make candle shades of carton paper, or how to decorate paper shades with cut-outs from chintz to tone with a room ('cutting out birds and flowers is a fascinating task, and one which is occupying a great many women'). For dining, candles with shades prevailed, with the candles sometimes mounted on springs so that as they burned down, they were continually pushed up towards the opening in the top of the shade.

The rising middle class, in their attempts to emulate their betters, discovered a style for their homes which has been the basis for middle-class respectability in England and many other parts of the world ever since.

*Edwardian designers'
imaginations ran riot with
lampshades in silk, chintz,
cretonne and paper as well as in
the traditional glass. According
to Hermann Muthesius, the
English invented and perfected
the silk shade, covering even
their candle flames with them.
The geometric glass table lamps
here show the influence of the
American Frank Lloyd Wright.*

Chapter 6

The Garden

I think heroic deeds were all conceived in the open air,
and all free poems also,
I think I could stop here and do miracles...
Now I see the secret of the making of the best persons –
It is to grow in the open air, and sleep with
the earth.

Walt Whitman, 'Song of the Open Road' from Leaves of Grass, 1867

During the Victorian age interest in gardens and gardening grew as new plants were discovered in the Far East, Australasia and the Americas. The Royal Horticultural Society, founded as the Horticultural Society of London in 1804, and the Royal Botanic Gardens at Kew, handed over to the nation in 1841, both added their weight to the exploration and research that was being undertaken. At the same time hybridizers, using more scientific methods than had been possible before, worked to produce new and better strains both of the recently arrived plants and of old ones such as roses.

Gardening was no longer the preserve of the very rich who had their garden designers, or of the very poor whose kitchen gardens were a necessity of life. Improved transport brought the produce of the countryside to the urban middle class, leaving these people free to pursue flower gardening as a hobby.

Another factor to encourage the interest in gardening among the middle classes was the introduction of conservatories and greenhouses. The availability of cheaper glass had made it one of the exciting building materials of the day. Joseph Paxton first designed the huge conservatory at Chatsworth, then the Crystal Palace that housed the Great Exhibition of the Industry of All Nations in 1851. In the wake of Crystal Palace, Victorians everywhere attached conservatories to their homes and built greenhouses in their gardens. Now the middle classes could grow tender and exotic specimens where before it had been the preserve of the rich, with their orangeries and heated glasshouses.

The influence of the Crystal Palace did not stop there. Moved to Sydenham once the Great Exhibition was over, the Crystal Palace was re-erected in a huge park, also designed by Paxton. A painting of the site by James Duffield Harding exhibited at the Royal Academy in 1854, shows a vulgar conglomeration of those very features that the wealthy landowners and entrepreneurs of the day were demanding of their garden designers.For many Victorians, reacting against the apparent naturalness of the landscape parks of Capability Brown in the eighteenth century, the park at Crystal Palace was the height of good garden design. The over-ornamentation that characterized their homes had crept into their gardens too.

The features of large gardens and public parks such as this were copied everywhere, even in suburban back gardens. There were terraces and balustrades with urns, and parterres with elaborate formal beds planted with bright carpets of flowers, often all of one colour or variety. Plants were raised in greenhouses, bedded out when they reached the peak of perfection and removed as soon as they were past their best, a labour-intensive operation only made possible by the abundant supply of cheap labour. Sometimes artifice was carried even further and beds were filled with coloured chippings instead of plants. Circular beds were especially popular, as were beds that showed off specimens of the newly arrived exotic plants of the day. Winding gravel paths led off in all directions, sometimes to a shrubbery, sometimes to a rockery ornamented with shells and garden gnomes.

By the 1870s garden designers began to react against so much artificiality. The Arts and Crafts Movement, whose influence was being felt in the realms of art, architecture and interior decoration, inspired a response in the world of garden design too. Harking back to earlier ages of English gardening, the reaction to the Crystal Palace style split into two opposing camps. On the one hand were those who, led by the great gardener William Robinson, looked to the vernacular tradition and the old style of cottage gardens, while on the other were those led by the architect Sir Reginald Blomfield, who found their inspiration in the formal gardens of the past.

The architecture-led camp brought about a revival of interest in French parterres, in the marble statuary of Italian gardens and in the old English art of topiary. Fanciful-shaped flowerbeds and gravel paths were once more in fashion, but now there appeared to be greater historical accuracy than in the middle of the century. Bedding-out continued as a feature, but with more variety in the plants used than previously, enabling it to be carried out almost year-round. Parterres were sometimes planted with conifers, dwarf oak might be used as an edging, low-growing foliage plants carpeted geometric beds, and spring bulbs filled beds that had once been left bare in the early part of the year. Standard fuchsias, heliotrope, weeping roses and sweet peas added height to the plantings, along with spiky and ball-headed plants. Sir Frank Crisp's gardens at Friar Park in 1910 summed up the mood of historic revivalism with their knot garden, Elizabethan garden, herb garden, Dutch garden and Bocaccio garden.

Meanwhile, William Robinson, who had referred to the bedding-out of plants as 'pastry-work gardening', led the natural

Designs for some conservatories and garden furniture carried on the elaborate, sometimes grotesque trends of the Victorians, but simplicity was gradually creeping in. Wicker and bamboo furniture which had been fashionable for indoor use in the Aesthetic period found its way back to the garden as an alternative to ornate and uncomfortable cast-iron. The vernacular revival brought a return to simple square-cut wooden garden furniture, like these two designs showing the influence of Voysey. The conservatory below, with its steep tiled and gabled roof and half-timbering is pure Edwardian fantasy - a suburban villa transported to the back garden.

school of gardening with his book *The English Flower Garden*, first published in 1883. The old English cottage garden with its enclosing wall or hedge suited perfectly the Arts and Crafts view of the importance of the relationship between house and garden. Informal borders of perennials, fruit trees and paths of stamped earth, brick or stone characterized the traditional cottage garden and were taken up with enthusiasm by Robinson and his followers in opposition to Blomfield and his. The gardens of Shakespeare's time and old herb gardens were another source of inspiration, with herb gardens becoming a decorative feature in their own right, and not simply an adjunct to a kitchen garden.

The Edwardian gardener of the time who most successfully managed to combine the natural style with carefully drawn garden plans was Gertrude Jekyll and she, together with Edwin Lutyens the architect, formed a partnership that was to influence garden design throughout the Edwardian period and on to the present day. Jekyll's special talent came from the fact that she had been trained as a painter, having enrolled at the Kensington School of Art in 1861. Failing eyesight prevented her from pursuing a career as an artist, so she turned instead to gardening. The form and colour of flowers were particularly important to her, as were the relationships that developed when different colours and shapes were juxtaposed. She preferred her plants to grow in informal drifts rather than in formal blocks, but since colour relationships were so important, a border still needed careful planning, often starting at one end with pale tones, moving through lilacs and blues to reach a climax of reds and yellows in the centre, and fading away gently to pale tones again at the other end.

The idea of perennial borders was quickly taken up by garden writers of the day and was passed on to the middle-class gardening public. For these people it was an idea that could not have come at a more opportune moment. The old-fashioned bedding-out style of gardening had been too labour-intensive and now that cheap labour was hard to come by, most people either had no gardener at all, or only a part-time one. *Everywoman's Encyclopaedia* of 1911 published Jekyll-inspired border plans that would have struck fear into the hearts of gardeners fifty years before, but they were plans that a modern middle-class household could put into effect at a modest cost.

The new garden styles suited the Edwardian passion for lightness and simplicity and their obsession with health and the open air. Weekend cottages provided a refuge from the noise and dust of town life, and the gardening correspondents of the day recommended small paved courtyards adjoining the cottage, partly roofed-in to protect against bad weather, but otherwise covered in light trellis 'over which charming roses, honeysuckles, jasmines and other creepers climb and cast a light shade without excluding the fresh country air'. In fact the Edwardian age might be described as the age of the climbing rose, for whereas nowadays there are approximately twenty climbing roses available, in those days there were a hundred and fifty or so.

Gardens were now being described as 'open-air rooms', a concept that was easier to grasp if the wallpapers used in one's house were covered with roses and honeysuckle scrambling up a wooden trellis. There was also a vogue for open-air bedrooms, permanent structures of wood, felting and corrugated iron with one completely open side. People were encouraged to sleep here even in winter: 'It is a mistake to think that the climate of this country is unsuitable for sleeping out in the winter. If armed with a hot-water bottle and warm clothing, one need never suffer from the cold.'

Inspired by Gertrude Jekyll and the natural school, people planted for a succession of colour throughout the year rather than for bold splashes only at the height of the summer, and one-colour gardens and wild-flower gardens also became popular. Scented and herb gardens found favour too, particularly as the ladies' skirts could brush against the plants as they passed, releasing their scent into the air. Little pots of thyme or basil here and there might recall old Italian gardens.

Serenity and harmony were the main requirements and the garden was to be enjoyed from the low, wide windows of the house as well as from the outside. The multiplicity of meandering Victorian garden paths were replaced with one or two straight paths, often taking their cue from the main windows of the house, or from a wide terrace. According to Gordon Allen in *The Cheap Cottage and Small House* of 1919, 'a multiplication of meaningless walks' was 'always to be avoided'. Focal points were framed by an arch or a pergola, or a path might lead to a summerhouse, sundial or bench with a background of evergreens. If space permitted, different areas of the garden might be given over to different activities such as tennis or croquet, or to a sunken lawn, but the aim would still be a single, harmonious whole.

Kitchen gardens were no longer economic, but they were convenient, so many people, at least in the country, still had one. A kitchen garden with a small orchard was, of course, a highly desirable accompaniment to a country cottage.

OPPOSITE PAGE: *Faithful reproductions of late-Victorian and Edwardian conservatories are readily available. They would have been used for informal sitting and for raising exotic plants.*

LEFT, ABOVE: *This conservatory is shaded by cane blinds that are in keeping with the period.*
APPEAL BLINDS

LEFT, BELOW: *The designer of this North American turn-of-the-century conservatory has exploited the exciting possibilities of stained glass to the full. English designers would have been more inclined to use plain glass panels, leaving the plants to take centre stage.*

Contrived international and historical styles were also tried out, with a fashion for Japanese gardens and for sunken bulb gardens in a supposedly Dutch style. *Everywoman's Encyclopaedia* even suggests a small orchard irregularly planted in imitation of an Italian hillside, or a roof garden following the 'example that a great firm has given, by having a large tea-garden above their shop in Oxford Street'.

The Edwardians continued the Victorian practice of conservatory gardening. The ever-popular orchids could be grown in a conservatory or special orchid house, while the conservatory also suited the revival of interest in cactus-growing. A conservatory could, of course, compensate for a lack of garden flowers during the winter months, or it could be exploited to its full potential as a year-round garden.

Gardening had not only become respectable for the middle classes, but had also become an acceptable occupation for a woman. Gertrude Jekyll was living proof of this, while Sussex boasted the Glynde School for Lady Gardeners. *Everywoman's Encyclopaedia* ran several articles on gardening as a career for women, stating in one that 'the profession of "jobbing gardening", if only it could be given a more picturesque and descriptive name, could be a pleasant and elevating profession for a lady of artistic ideas'.

While stiffness and formality were on the wane in private gardens, in public parks they were still very much to the fore. The tradition of carpet bedding persisted, despite the huge cost, though it was stopped in Hyde Park in 1904. For a public garden in an inner-city area, bedding was more or less essential as a way of keeping the gardens looking fresh. In Philips Park in Manchester, seven thousand trees and shrubs had to be replaced annually because of the effects of pollution. Carpet bedding in parks reached new heights of artifice with the introduction of three-dimensional or sculptural bedding. In 1907 Pearson Park in Hull featured a roll of stair carpet with a length unrolled, the whole thing made of living plants, while for the coronation of George V, floral crowns appeared in many public parks. Municipal gardens of the early twentieth century were also home to bowling greens, edged with alpines or herbaceous plants, and some municipal gardens featured old-fashioned gardens in an Elizabethan or William and Mary style.

Eventually another strand of fashion in garden design began to take root, developing from the Georgian revival in architecture. Neo-Georgian homes as designed by Lutyens needed neo-classical gardens to go with them. Characterized by restrained symmetry, broad vistas and an openness that flew in the face of the Arts and Crafts garden, the neo-classical garden needed a 'landscape architect' – a term first coined by Thomas Mawson in the 1890s – for its design. According to Brent Elliott in 1986 in *Victorian Gardens*, people were not yet ready for a return to the open landscape parks of the eighteenth century, for these were too different from Victorian gardens to be acceptable. However, he likens the golf courses of the early years of the twentieth century to the eighteenth-century landscape parks and ends his survey of Victorian gardening by saying how, 'with an exquisite irony, the Victorian garden completed its circular progress. The rebellion against the eighteenth-century landscape park at the beginning of the nineteenth century had resulted in attempts to bring back the gardening styles of the past, and after a century in this historical revivalism, the movement ended by resurrecting the very style it had begun by reacting against.' The same may be said to be true of the architecture as well.

STOCKISTS

The lists of suppliers given on these pages cannot be exhaustive and are intended only as a starting point. Local papers and commercial telephone directories are always worth looking at and are good sources of information about your own area. Alternatively there are many organisations giving specialist information and advice and those who will search for specific items.

UNITED KINGDOM

FINISHES
Art Veneers Co Ltd
Industrial Estate,
Mildenhall,
Suffolk IP28 7AY

John Boddy's Fine Wood
  and Tool Store,
Riverside Sawmills
Boroughbridge
N Yorks YO5 9LJ

PANELLING
Blamphayne Oak
Blamphanye Farm
Northleigh
Nr Colyton
Devon EX13 6BY

Bylaw
The Old Mill
Brookend
Ross-on-Wye
Herefordshire
HR9 7EE

and
5 Merchants Court
St George's Street
Norwich
Norfolk NR3 1AB

Deacon and Sandys
Hillcrest Farm Oast
Hartley
Cranbrook
Kent TN17 3QD

Heritage Oak
Unit VI
Dean Clough Industrial
  Park
Halifax HX3 5AX

Stuart Interiors
Barring Court
Barrington
Ilminster
Somerset TA19 0NQ

KITCHENS
Crabtree Kitchens
The Twickenham Centre
Norcutt Road
Twickenham TW2 6SR

Hygrove
152-154 Merton Road
Wimbledon
London SW19 1EH

Andrew Mackintosh
  Kitchens
Units 1-2 Grenfell Place
Maidenhead
Berkshire SL6 1HL

Owles Kitchens
OwlesWarehouse
4 Trinity Street
Bungay
Suffolk NR35 1EH

Pennybee Interiors
53-54 High Street
Wimbledon Village
London SW19

Robinson & Cornish
The Old Tannery
Swimbridge
Devon EX32 0PL

Smallbone of Devizes
Hopton Workshop
The London Road
Devizes
Wilts SN10 2EU

The Suffolk Journeyman
2 Pytches Road
Woodbridge
Suffolk 1P12 1EP

TIMBER MOULDINGS
Bristol Design Ltd
14 Perry Road
Bristol BS1 5BG

Richard Burbidge Ltd
Whittington Road
Oswestry
Shropshire SY1 1HZ

A W Champion
Champion House
Burlington Road
New Malden
Surrey

Tony Murland
78 High Street
Needham Market
Ipswich
Suffolk IP6 8AW

W F Newson & Sons Ltd
61 Pimlico Road
London
SW1W 8NF

Winther Browne & Co Ltd
Nobel Road
Eley Estate
Edmonton
London N18 3DX

RADIATORS
Bisque
244 Belsize Road
London NW6 4BT

MHS Radiators Ltd
35 Nobel Square
Burnt Mills Industrial
  Estate
Basildon
Essex SS13 1 LT

Radiating Style
194 New Kings Road
London SW6 4NF

Vogue (UK) Ltd
Unit 1, Tower Street
Pelham Street
Wolverhampton
WV3 0BW

STOVES & COOKERS
Coalbrookdale
  (Aga-Rayburn)
PO Box 30
Ketley
Telford
Shropshire TF1 4DD

Dovre Castings
  (also Franco Belge)
Unit 1, Weston Works
Weston Lane
Tyseley
Birmingham B11 3RP\

Smith & Wellstood
  Esse Ltd
Bonnybridge
Stirlingshire
FK4 2AP

Vermont Castings
1-7 Smythe Road
Bristol BS3 2BX

ARCHITECTURAL SALVAGE
Andy Thornton
  Architectural Antiques
Victoria Mills, Stainland
Greetland, Halifax
West Yorkshire
HX4 8AD

Architectural Antiques
1 York Street
Bedford MK40 3RJ

Architectural Heritage
  of Leicester
107-109 Highcross St
Leicester

Baileys Architectural
  Antiques
The Engine Shed
Ashburton Industrial
  Estate
Ross-on-Wye
Herefordshire
HR9 7BW

Cardiff Reclamation
The Jardinerie Garden
  Centre
Newport Road
St Mellons
Cardiff CF3 9XH

Conservation Building
  Products Ltd
Forge Lane,
Cradley Heath
Warley
West Midlands
B64 5AL

Dorchester Reclamation
Midway Down Farm
Copyhold Lane
Winterbourne Abbas
Dorchester
Dorset DT2 9LT

Drummonds's of
  Bramley
Birtley Farm
Horsham Road
Bramley
Guildford GU5 0LA

Edinburgh Architectural
  Salvage Yard
Unit 6
Couper Street (off Cobury
  Street)
Leith
Edinburgh EH6 6HH

Hammonds
27 Monkstown Farm
Monkstown
Dublin

Lasco
Mark Street (off Paul
  Street)
London EC2A 4ER

Nostalgia
61 Shaw Heath
Stockport
Cheshire SK3 8BH

Solopark
The Old Railway Station
Station Road
Nr Pampisford
Cambs CB2 4HB

Tobys
Merriot House
Hennock Road, Exeter
Devon

Walcot Reclamation
The Yard
108 Walcot Street
Bath BA1 5BG

Wells Reclamation
The Old Cider Farm
Wells Road
Coxley, nr Wells
Somerset BA5 1RQ

BATHROOMS -
REPRODUCTION
Armitage Shanks Ltd
Armitage
Rugeley
Staffs WS15 4BT

BC Sanitan
12 Nimrod Way
Elgar Road
Reading
Berks RG2 0EB

Brass & Traditional
  Sinks
Devanden Green
Nr Chepstow
Gwent NP6 6PL

Czech & Speake Ltd
Cambridge Heath Road
London E2 9DA

Doulton Bathrooms
Lawton Road
Alsager
Stoke-on-Trent
Staffs ST7 2DF

Heritage Bathrooms
Unit 1A Princess Street
Bristol BS3 4AG

Imperial Bathrooms
Imperial Buildings
Northgate Way
Aldridge
Walsall
West Midlands
WS9 8SR

Original Bathrooms
143-145 Kew Road
Richmond-on-Thames
Surrey TW9 2PN

Pipe Dreams
72 Gloucester Road
London SW7 4QT

Sitting Pretty
131 Dawes Road
London SW6 7EA

Vernon Tutbury
PO Box 193
Hilton
Denley DE6 5WW

Twyfords
Caradon Bathrooms Ltd
PO Box 23
Shelton New Road
Cliffe Vale
Stoke-on-Trent
ST4 7AL

BATHROOMS -
ORIGINAL
Bathshield (Repro and
  Original)
Blenheim Studio
Forest Row
Sussex RH18 5EZ

Bygone Bathrooms
39 Honor Oak Park
London SE23 1DZ

Nostalgia Bathrooms
61 Shaw Heath
Stockport
Cheshire SK3 8DH

The Water Monopoly
16-18 Lonsdale Road
London NW6 6RD

RADIATORS
Bisque
244 Belsize Road
London NW6 4BT

MHS Radiators Ltd
35 Nobel Square
Burnt Mills Industrial
  Estate
Basildon
Essex SS13 1LT

Radiating Style
194 New Kings Road
London SW6 4NF

Vogue (UK) Ltd
Unit 1, Tower Street,
Pelham Street
Wolverhampton
WV3 0BW

IRONWORK
R Bleasdale & Co
394 Caledonian Road
London N1 1DW

G W Day & Co
East Chiltington Forge
Highbridge Lane
South Chailey
Lewes
East Sussex BN7 3QY

TILES/FLOORING
Areen Stonecraft Ltd
Unit 11
Harwarden Industrial
  Park
Manor Lane
Harwarden
Deeside
Clwyd CH5 3PP

A Bell & Co
Thornton Road
Kingsthorpe
Northampton NN2 6LT

Chameleon Slate Flooring
  Co Ltd
Unit 2a
Moorfield Industrial
  Estate
Yeadon
Leeds
LS19 7BN

Frome Reclamation
Grants Yard
Willowvale
Frome BA11 1BG

Mandarin
Grange Mill
Raglan
Gwent NP5 2AA

Paris Ceramics Ltd
583 Kings Road
London SW6 2EH

Star Ceramics
75 Lower Sloane Street
London SW1W 8DA

Wellington Tile Co
Tonedale Industrial Estate
Milverton
Wellington
Somerset TA21 0AZ

STAIRCASES/BALUSTERS
Allchurch & Reeve
128 Claremont Avenue
New Malden
Surrey KT3 6QS

Richard Burbidge Ltd
Whittington Road
Oswestry
Shropshire
SY11 1HZ

Robert Coles furniture
  & joinery
Church House
Broad Street
Congresbury
Avon

Gifford Mead
533 Kings Road
London SW10 0TZ

Hapfo Pollards Ltd
1 Ware Hall Industrial
  Estate
Salford
Milton Keynes
MK17 3AZ

JAK Products
Glebe Cottage
Hunsingore
nr Wetherby
N Yorks LS22 5HY

Mounts Hill Woodcraft
  & Design
Paynetts Lane
Goldhurst
Kent TN1 1DY

W H Newson
61 Pimlico Road
London SW1 8NF

Theresa Spinks
Cherub House
Market Place
Wolsingham
Co Durham DL13 3AB

Winther Browne Ltd
Nobel Road
Eley Estate
Edmonton
London N18 3DX

LIGHTING
Albert Bartram
177 Hivings Hill
Chesham
Buckinghamshire
HP5 2PN

Andy Thornton
Ainleys Industrial
    Estate,
Elland
Yorkshire HX5 9JP

Ann's
34a/b Kensington
    Church Street
London W8 4HA

Antique & Decorative
    Lighting Dealers
    Association
Littleton House
Littleton
Somerset TA11 6NP

Ashley & Rock Ltd
Morecambe Road
Ulverston
Cumbria LA12 9BN

Besselink & Jones
99 Walton Street
London SW3 2HH

Best & Lloyd Ltd
William Street West
Smethwick, Warley
West Midlands
B66 2NX

Michel Bouillot
Trinity Wine
82A Acre Lane
London SW2 5QN

Chelsom
Unit 4
Hurlingham Business
    Park
Sullivan Road
London SW6 3DU

Classic Reproductions
Unit 16
Highams Lodge
    Business Centre
Blackhorse Lane
London E17 6SH

Dernier & Hamlyn
47/48 Berners Street
London W1P 3AD

Elite Lighting
18 Bromley Hill
Bromley
Kent BR1 4JX

The End of Day Lighting
    Company
54 Parkway
London NW1 7AH

Fritz Fryer Decorative
    Antique Lighting
12 Brookend Street
Ross-on-Wye
Herefordshire
HR9 7EG

John Cullen Lighting
216 Fulham Palace Road
London W6 9NT

Lighting Association
Stafford Park
Telford
Shropshire TF3 3BD

Magic Lanterns
    By George
23 George Street
St Albans
Hertfordshire AL3 4ES

Marston & Langinger
George Edwards Road
Fakenham
Norfolk NR 21 8NL

Stiffkey Lamp Shop
Stiffkey
nr Wells-Next-Sea
Norfolk NR23 1AJ

Temple Lighting
Stockwell House
1 Stockwell Lane
Wavendon
Milton Keynes MK17 8LS

Tempus Stet
Trinity Business Centre
305-309 Rotherhithe
    Street
London SE16 1EY

Christopher Wray
600 King's Road
London SW6 2DX

**WALLPAPERS AND
FABRICS**
G P & J Baker
PO Box 30, West End
    Road
High Wycombe
Bucks HP11 2QD

Cole & Son
    (Wallpapers)
18 Mortimer Street
London W1N 7RD

Marvic Textiles
12 Mortimer Street
London W1

Christopher Moore
1 Munroe Terrace
London SW10 0DL

H A Percheron
97/9 Cleveland Street
London W1P 5PN

Sandersons
53 Berners Street
London W1

Warner Fabrics
Bradbourne Drive
Tilbrook
Milton Keynes
MK7 8BE

John Wilman Fabrics &
    Wallpapers
Culshaw Street
Burnley
Lancs
For stockists ring

Zoffany
63 South Audley Street
London
W1Y 5BF

WINDOWS
Award Windows
    Limited
Brue Way
Highbridge
Somerset TA9 4AW

Classic Designs
Unit 15 Bilton Industrial
    Estate
Humber Avenue
Coventry CV3 1JL

The Cotswold Casement
    Company
Fielding Works
London Road
Moreton-in-Marsh
Gloucestershire
GL56 0HH

Crittal Windows
Springwood Drive
Braintree
Essex CM7 7YN

The Forge
G Glass
Blackmoorfoot Road
Crosland Hill
Huddersfield HD4 7AA

Lattice Windows
Fiddington Farm
Monks Lane
Fiddington
Gloucestershire
GL20 7BJ

The London Crown
    Glass Company
Pyghtle House
Misbourne Avenue
Gerrards Cross
Buckinghamshire
SL0 0PD

Middlesex Glass
2 South Street
Old Isleworth
Middlesex TW7 7BG

The Original Box Sash
    Window Company
Freepost
Windsor
Berks SL4 1BR

J Scott (Thompson)
Bridge Street
Thrapston
Northants NN14 4LR

C R Smith
27 Gardeners Street
Dunfermline
Fife
KY12 0RN

Stained Glass & Period
   Glazing Co
Warryfield Barn
Walford
Ross-on-Wye
Herefordshire

Ventrolla
51 Tower Street
Harrogate HG1 1H5

DOORS
British Gates & Timber
Castletons Oak Sawmills
Biddendon
Nr Ashford
Kent

Classic Designs
Unit 15
Bilton Industrial Estate
Humber Avenue
Coventry CV3 1JL

Clayton-Munroe
Kingston
Staverton
Totnes
Devon

Forgeries
The Old Butchery
High Street
Twyford
Hants

Kirkpatrick Ltd
PO Box 17
Frederick Street
Wallsall
W Midlands

The London Door
   Company
165 St Johns Hill
London SW11 1TQ

Marston & Langinger
192 Ebury Street
London
SW1W 8UP

Sussex Oak Doors
Swan House
39 High Street
Billingshurst
W Sussex

CONSERVATORIES
Abbeydale Conservatories
Hewell Road
Redditch
Worcester B97 6AR

Amdega Limited
Faverdale
Darlington
Co Durham DL3 0PW

Appeal Blinds Ltd
16 Barnack Centre
Novers Hill
Bedminster
Bristol BS3 5QE

Bartholomew
   Conservatories
5 Haslemere Industrial
   Estate
Haslemere
Surrey GU27 1DW

Glass Houses
63 Islington Park Street
London N1 1QB

Holloways
Lower Court
Suckley
Worcestershire WR6 5DE

Oak Leaf Conservatories
   Limited
Clifton Common
   Industrial Park
Kettlestring Lane
York YO3 8XF

Portland Conservatories
Freepost
Manchester M5 3GL

Regal Conservatories
Dept 1C
Cromford Road
Langley Mill
Notts NG16 4EB

Westbury Conservatories
   Limited
Martels
High Easter Road
Barnston
Essex CM6 1NA

USA

ARCHITECTURAL SALVAGE
ADI
2045 Broadway
Kansas City
MO 64108

Architectural Salvage
   Cooperative
1328 East 12th Street
Davenport
IA 52803

Architectural Salvage
   Warehouse
337 Berry Street
Brooklyn
New York
NY 11211

Great American Salvage
34 Cooper Square
New York
NY 10003

Housewreckers NB
   & Salvage Co
396 Somerset Street
New Brunswick
NJ 08901

Kayne & Son
Custom Forged Hardware
76 Daniel Ridge Road
Candler
NC 28715

New Boston Building
   Wrecking Co Inc
84 Arsenal Street
Watertown
MA 02172

Off the Wall
Architectural Antiques
950 Glenneyre Street
Laguna Beach
CA 92651

Old Home Building
   & Restoration
PO Box 384
West Suffield
CT 06093

Old House-New House
   Restoration
169 N Victoria Street
St Paul
MN 55104

Omega Salvage
2406 San Pablo Avenue
Berkeley
CA 94702

Pagliacco Turning &
   Milling
PO Box 225
Woodacre
CA 94973

Pasternak's Emporium
2515 Morse Street
Houston
TX 77019

Price & Viser Millwork
2536 Valencia Street
Bellingham
WA 98226

Red Baron's
6320 Roswell Road
Atlanta
GA 30328

Renovator's
PO Box 2515
Dept 9940
Conway
NH 03818-2515

Roland Millwork
   & Lumber
393 North Pearl Street
Albany
NY 12207

Salvage One
1524 S Sangamon Street
Chicago
IL 60608

Second Chance
230 7th Street
Macon
GA 31202

Shakertown Corporation
PO Box 400
Winlock
WA 98596

Silver Creek Mill
Englers Block
1335 W Hwy 76
Branson
MO 65616

The Smoot Lumber
   Company
PO Box 26188
1201 N Royal Street
Alexandria
VA 22313

Speciality Building
   Supply
PO Box 13529
Jackson
MS 39326

WALLCOVERINGS AND BLINDS
Bennington's
1271 Manheim Pike
Lancaster
PA 17601

Style Wallcovering
400 Galleria 400
Southfield
MI 48304

USA Blind Factory
1312 Live Oak
Houston
TX 77003

The Warner Company
108 S Desplaines
Chicago
IL 60661
and
6-136 The Merchandise
Mart, Chicago

Worldwide Wall-
   coverings & Blinds Inc
333 Stokie Blvd
Northbrook
IL 60062

WINDOWS & DOORS
Andersen Windows
PO Box 3900
Peoria
IL 61614

Marvin Windows
Warroad
MN 56763

Peachtree
PO Box 700
Norcross
GA 30091

BATHROOMS
The Chicago Faucet Co
2100 Clearwater Drive
Des Plaines
IL 60018

Danfoss Faucet Co
2 El Dorado Ct
Hampton
VA 23669

Eljer Plumbingware
PO Box 879001
Dallas
TX 75287-9001

Jason International
8328 Macarthur Drive
North Little Rock
AR 72118

Howard Kaplan
Bath Shop
47 E 12th Street
New York
NY 10003

Kohler Co
Kohler
WI 53044

Moen Inc
377 Woodland Ave
Elyria
OH 44036

Peerless Products
PO Box 2469
Shawnee Mission
KS 66201

KITCHENS
Aristokraft
PO Box 3513
Evansville
IN 47734-3513

Dacor
950 South Raymond
Avenue
Pasadena
CA 91109

European Kitchens
& Bath
San Diego CA
619 452 5092

Kitchen Aid
PO Box 558
St Joseph
MI 49085

Kitchens by Krengel
1688 Grand Ave
Minneapolis
MN 551105

Kohler Co
Dept IN3
Kohler
WI 53044

Kraftmaid Cabinetry
16052 Industrial Parkway
PO Box 1055
Middlefield
OH 44062

Merillat
KDP Kit Dept 4736
PO Box 1946
Adrian
MI 49221

Purcell Murray Co
113 Park Lane
Brisbane
CA 94005

Rohl Corporation
1559 Sunland Lane
Costa Mesa
CA 92626

Snaidero International
201 132nd Street
Los Angeles
CA 90061

Wellborn Cabinet Inc
PO Box 1210
Rt 1, Hwy 77
S Ashland
AL 36251

LIGHTING
Georgia Lighting Supply
Co Inc
520 14th Street NW
Atlanta
GA 30318

Illustrious Lighting
1925 Fillmore Street
San Francisco
CA 94115

Rejuvenation Lamp
& Fixture Co
1100 S E Grand Avenue
Portland
Oregon 97214

Unique Art Glass Co Inc
5060 Arsenal
St Louis
Missouri 63139

FIREPLACES
Eric Anthony
Reproductions
8730 Santa Monica
Boulevard
PO Box 69686
Los Angeles
CA 90069

Architectural Antiques Ltd
of Little Rock
1321 E Second
Little Rock
AR 72202

Bennington Bronze
PO Box 183
Woodbury
CT 06798

Freestanding Fireplaces
Inc
Route 52
Jeffersonville
NY 12748

Ye Old Mantel Shoppe
3800 NE Second Avenue
Miami
FL 33137

TILES AND FLOORING
Antique Floors
Dallas
TX
214 760 9330

Boen Hardwood Flooring
Rt 2
Bowles Industrial Park
Hollie Drive
Martinsville
VA 24112

Carminart
Elmsford NY
914 592 6330

Design Tile Inc
Tyson Corners VA
703 734 2551

Facings of America
Phoenix AZ
603 955 5092

French-Brown Floors
Dallas TX
214 363 4341

CANADA

BATHROOMS
Bathrooms & Dreams Inc
225 The East Mall
Etobicoke
233 4704

Bathtub King
4615 Burgoyne
625 6734

W C Finebath & Kitchens
450 South Service West
Oakville
338 3303

Neto Bathrooms Inc
5129 Tomken
624 0628

DOORS
Classic Entrance
159 Wilkinsons Road
Unit 7
Brampton
455 5500

Classic Millwork Co Ltd
Britannia West
564 9705

Doorland
65 Bowes Road
Concord
Ontario
736 1787

Dundas Doors Inc
800 Dundas Street East
Mississauga
Ontario
896 1448

Overhead Door
RR4
PO Box 2075
Brockville
342 3139

W M Willie Moller
Industries Ltd
2550 Golden Ridge Road
Unit 6
Mississauga
Ontario
949 4935

KITCHENS
Cobol Kitchens Inc
215 Carling View Drive
204 Etobicoke
675 3098

Kitchenworld
321 Supertest Road
Mississauga
663 2363

Markow & Associates Ltd
133 Wilson at Rebecca
Oakville
842 1502

Milano Kitchens Ltd
1325 Eglinton Avenue
   East
Dixie
Mississauga
238 1144

Millcraft Kitchen
   Cabinet Ltd
145 Traders Boulevard
   East
Unit 8
Mississauga
568 3111

STAINED GLASS
Andreas Mladek
Creative Glass Work
1285 Crown
Vancouver
British Columbia

Architectural Warehouse
PO Box 3065
Station D
Ottawa K1P 6H6

Artistic Touch of Glass
3010B Arlington
Saskatoon
Saskatchewan

Celtic Art Glass
228 Hollyberry Trail
Willowdale
Ontario M2H 2P4

Fantasy in Glass
   Glassworks
703 The Queensway
Toronto
Ontario
M8Y 1L2

Glassmiths Studio
12730 127th Street
Edmonton
Alberta

Lakefield Stained Glass
8 Burnham Street
Lakefield
Ontario

Pacific Glass Works
7709 Royal Oak Avenue
Burnaby
British Columbia
V5J 4K2

Prairie Stained Glass
587 Sargent Avenue
Winnipeg
Manitoba
R3D 1W6

Winter Art Glass Studio
16010-118 Avenue
Edmonton
Alberta T5V 1C6

AUSTRALIA

STOVES & FIREPLACES
Coonara
Ferntree Gully
Victoria
03 758 6666

Fireking
Seven Hills
NSW
02 674 4444

Homemaker Products
Virginia
Qld
07 265 7133

Lasting Impressions
593 Burwood Road
Hawthorn
Victoria 3122
03 819 1170

Masport
Silverwater
NSW
02 644 6188

Old Balgowlah
   Restorations
377 Sydney Road
Balgowlah 2093

The Old Sydney
   Renovation Co
51 Darling Street
Cnr Nicholson Street
Balmain East Sydney
02 818 1683

Total Energy
Castle Hill
NSW
02 634 5911

STAINED GLASS
Lance Feeney
Surry Hills
Sydney
NSW

A E Harradence & Co
Sydney
NSW

Stained Glass Overlay
Bathurst
NSW
06 331 7483

Stained Glass Overlay
Albion
QLD
07 262 7605

Stained Glass Overlay
Bendigo
Victoria
05 441 3093

Stained Glass Overlay
Parahills West
SA
08 258 4425

Stained Glass Overlay
Claremont
WA
09 384 7535

DOOR FURNITURE
Gainsborough Hardware
   Industries Ltd
275 Canterbury Road
Canterbury 3126
Victoria
03 836 0211

House of Knobs
101 Union Road
Surrey Hills
Melbourne
Victoria 3127
03 898 4782

Mother of Pearl & Sons
72A Oxford Street
Paddington
NSW 2021
02 332 4455

ARCHITECTURAL SALVAGE & ANTIQUES
Agnews Architectural
   Antiques
215 Swan Street
Richmond
Victoria 3121
03 428 0583 - 429 3438

The Antique Garden
438 Chapel Street
South Yarra 3141
03 241 7701

TILES
Renditions
49 Trafalgar Street
Annandale
02 516 4066

Rogers Seller & Mynhill
27 City Road
South Melbourne
Victoria 3205
03 62 0781

Signorino Ceramics
843-851
Sydney Road
Brunswick
Victoria 3056
03 383 1788

IRONWORK
The Fence Factory
99 Dunheved Circuit
St Marys
NSW 2760
02 673 3788

The Furphy Foundry
PO Box 1390
Shepparton
Victoria 3630
05 821 2422

Melbourne Aluminium &
   Iron Lacework
452 Heidelberg Road
Fairfield
Victoria 3078
03 489 5100

Peter Baker-Finch
Cnr Ipswich Road & Clive
   Street
Annerley
Brisbane
07 892 3544

Predictions Pty Ltd
46-50 King Street
Prahran 3181
Victoria
03 529 4488

CONSERVATORIES & GAZEBOS
The Conservatory
62 Unley Road
Unley
SA
08 272 9657

The Garden Room
Adele's of Melbourne
03 899 6325

Gazebo World
Lot 31
Koala Way
Horsley Park 2162
02 620 1495

The Gazebo Works
Robertson
NSW 2577
048 85 1328

INDEX

Bibliography

Allen, Gordon, *The Cheap Cottage and Small House: A Manual of Economical Building* (Batsford, 6th ed., 1919)

Barrett, Helen and Phillips, John, *Suburban Style: The British Home, 1840-1960* (Macdonald Orbis, 1987)

Beales, Peter, *Edwardian Rose*s (Jarrold, 1979)

Brown, Jane *The Art and Architecture of English Gardens* (Weidenfeld & Nicolson, 1989)

Calloway, Stephen, *The House of Liberty: Masters of Style and Decoration* (Thames & Hudson, 1992)

Cornforth, John 'Manderston, Berwichshire', article in *Country Life*, 26 August 1993

Elder-Duncan, J.H., *The House Beautiful and Useful* (Cassell & Co., 1907)

Elliot, Brent, *Victorian Gardens* (Batsford, 1986)

Everywoman's Encyclopaedia (publisher unknown, Bouverie Street, London, 1911)

Fleming, Laurence and Gore, Alan, *The English Garden* (Michael Joseph, 1979)

Garden City Houses and Domestic Interior Details (The Architectural Press, 4th ed., 1924)

Girouard, Mark, *Life in the English Country House* (Yale University Press, 1979)

Gloag, John and Mansfield, Leslie, *The House We Ought to Live In* (Duckworth, 1923)

Gore, Alan and Ann,. *The History of English Interiors* (Phaidon, 1991)

Hall, Michael, 'Eloquence of Line', article in *Country Life*, 19 August 1993

ed. Holme, Geoffrey, *'The Studio' Yearbook of Appl.ied Art,* ('The Studio', 1921)

Jellicoe, Goode and Lancaster, *The Oxford Companion to Gardens* (Oxford University Press, 1991)

Little Palaces: The Suburban House in North London, 1919-1939 (Middlesex Polytechnic, 1987)

Miller, Judith and Martin, *Period Details* (Mitchell Beazley, 1987)

Morris, William, *Hopes and Fears for Art: Five Lectures Delivered in Birmingham, London and Nottingham*, 1878-1881 (Longmans, Green & Co., 4th ed., 1896)

Muthesius, Hermann, *Das Englische Haus* (Translated by Janet Seligman, published by Granada Publishing Ltd, 1979)

Pevsner, Nikolaus, *Pioneers of Modern Design* (re. ed., Pelican, 1960)

Phillips, R. Randal *The Servantless House* (Country Life, 1920)

Service, Alistair, *Edwardian Interiors* (Barrie & Jenkins, 1982)

Sills, Spencer, *Common-Senmse Homes: A Practical Book for Everybody* (Cassell & Co., 1912)

Sutherland, W.G., *Stencilling for Craftsmen* (The Decorative Art Journals Co Ltd., Manchester)

Thornton, Peter, *Authentic Decor: The Domestic Interior*, 1620-1920 (Weidenfeld & Nicolson, 1984)

Turner, Tom, English Garden Design (Antique Collectors' Club, 1986)

Volpe, Tod M. and Cathers, Beth, *Treasures of the American Arts and Crafts Movement, 1890-1920*, (Thames & Hudson, 1988)

ed. Wright, Richardson, *Inside the House of Good Taste* (Robert McBride & Co., New York, 2nd ed., 1918)

Yesterday's Shopping: The Army & Navy Store Catalogue, 1907 (facsimile, David & Charles reprints, 1969)

Picture Credits